KARL MARX

KARL MARX

AN ILLUSTRATED BIOGRAPHY

Werner Blumenberg

Translated by Douglas Scott

VERSO
London · New York

First published by Rowohlt 1962

English translation first published 1972

This revised edition first published by Verso 1998

Picture credits: AKG, London (*pages 5, 34, 43, 75, 145*); David King (*pages 25, 64, 95, 105, 127, 131, 137, 160*); Mary Evans Picture Library (*pages 29, 93, 144*); all other pictures courtesy of the International Institute for Social History, Amsterdam

Verso
UK: 6 Meard Street, London W1V 3HR
USA: 180 Varick Street, New York, NY 10014–4606

Verso is the imprint of New Left Books

ISBN 1–85984–705–6

British Library Cataloguing in Publication Data
A catalogue record for this book is available from the British Library

Library of Congress Cataloging-in-Publication Data
A catalog record for this book is available from the Library of Congress

Designed and typeset by Lucy Morton & Robin Gable, Grosmont
Printed and bound in the United States by R.R. Donnelley & Sons

CONTENTS

FOREWORD

Werner Blumenberg was born in Germany in 1900. He was the son of a Protestant pastor and originally intended to study theology. As a student however, he became politically active and joined the German Social Democratic Party after the Kapp Putsch. He worked first as a miner and then between 1926 and 1933 as a journalist on various Social Democratic newspapers. He was active in the underground opposition to Hitler, both in Germany between 1933 and 1936 and in Holland after the Nazi invasion. He first became associated with the International Institute of Social History in 1940 and later became head of its German section. In addition to his biography of Marx, he made a number of important scholarly contributions to the history of the German workers' movement and produced a definitive edition of the Engels–Bebel correspondence. He continued working in the Institute until his death in 1965.

Blumenberg's biography of Marx was a direct outcome of his work at the Institute and drew upon sources only to be found in its collection. The Institute was founded in 1935 by the Dutch economic historian, N. W. Posthumus, with financial help provided by *De Centrale Arbeiders-Versekeringsbank* (the Central Workers' Insurance Company). Its original purpose was to provide a library which would house German socialist, anarchist and labour movement archives whose existence was threatened by the Nazi takeover in Germany. As National Socialism spread over German borders into Austria, Czechoslovakia and Poland, further deposits were added. By the time of the outbreak of the Second World War, the Institute had come to include the archives of the German Social Democratic Party with its unique Marx–Engels collection, and an incomparable cache of material relating to Bakunin and anarchist movements assembled by Max Nettlau.

In 1940 Amsterdam itself was overrun by the Nazis. The bulk of the library was removed to Germany and the building was sacked by the occupying forces. The archives however had already been dispersed and hidden for the duration of the war (much of the most valuable material was stored in Oxford). After 1945, the City of Amsterdam and the Dutch government took over some of the financial responsibility of the Institute and a proportion of the hidden collections was slowly reassembled. The Institute was officially reopened at the beginning of the 1950s and a grant from the Ford Foundation henceforward financed a catalogue of the collection. The Institute has now become part of the University of Amsterdam.

Blumenberg's biography of Marx was prepared in the late 1950s and published in 1962. Blumenberg was not a Marxist and his biography can be firmly situated in the Social Democratic tradition of writing on Marx (Nicolaevsky and Maenchen Helfen, Braunthal, Rubel, Cole, Laski). His account of Marx is scrupulous and well researched. Occasionally, however, his mode of approach results in misinterpretations. Most of these are relatively unimportant. In one case however, the treatment of Marx's relationship to the Commune, it is clear that Blumenberg's Social Democratic interpretation results in a serious misunderstanding of Marx's position. Blumenberg suggests that Marx not only mythologised the Commune by ignoring its practical limitations and the exceptional conditions under which it took place, but further that he was perfectly aware of 'the truth' ('the distortion fitted his political theory' [page 142 below]). Blumenberg backs up his juxtaposition of the real historical facts against Marx's conscious mythologization of them by a comparison between *The Civil War in France* and Marx's letter to Domela Nieuwenhuis in 1881 (p. 142).

This is to create a wholly false picture of Marx's conception of the Commune. Of course, as Blumenberg shows, Marx was well aware of the exceptional historical circumstances which produced the Commune. But Marx was not concerned so much with the historical specificity of the Commune as with the political form of government that it threw up – a type of *State* that would make it possible for the working-class at long last to accomplish the 'emancipation of labour'. In other words, the lesson which Marx drew from the Commune was political not social. Marx was under no illusion that the leadership of the Commune represented a fully-fledged socialist government. But he was insistent that the Commune was 'essentially a government of the working classes'. To suggest, as Blumenberg does, that the Commune's abolition of the distinction between legislative and executive and its decree that municipal officials should be paid workers' wages, were no more than 'emergency measures necessary in a besieged city' is to stretch historical credibility. Certainly neither of these measures had been enacted during the previous siege of Paris by the Prussians. It is difficult to see why Blumenberg should think that Marx's letter to Nieuwenhuis constitutes an implicit confession of previous mythologization. It is clear that Marx did not think that the emergence of the Commune provided a universal pattern of social revolution. But this had never been at issue in *The Civil War in France*. It is clear also that Marx considered that the Communards had made mistakes. (This was clear to Marx not only in 1881, but also at the time of the Commune itself.) But this was in no sense incompatible with his *political* defence of the Commune in *The Civil War in France*. Marx's letter to Nieuwenhuis was generally concerned with the historical preconditions of a transition to socialism. The central theme of his letter was: 'One thing you can at any rate be sure of; a socialist government does not come into power in a country unless conditions are so developed that it can immediately take the necessary measures for intimidating the mass of the bourgeoisie sufficiently to gain time – the first desideratum – for permanent action.' Thus the Nieuwenhuis letter certainly established the limits of historical possibility of the Commune and its exceptional character, but it can in no sense be used to confirm an accusation of conscious political distortion.

Blumenberg's primary aim however was not so much to write a political as a personal biography of Marx. The intention of the book was to get away from the hagiographic style which had marred earlier socialist biographies of Marx and to produce an uncensored account of the human Marx with all his human failings. In contrast to earlier studies, this book lays bare Marx's not infrequent callousness towards friends and supporters, his occasional dabbling in the seamier side of European diplomacy, his mercenary attitude to his relatives, his aspirations to a conventional bourgeois mode of life and conduct, with its characteristically hypocritical treatment of the problem of marital infidelity and illegitimate offspring. For the author rightly believed that to present a truthful and unadorned account of the human Marx in place of the stereotype Promethean demi-god, in no way detracted from Marx's greatness.

Paradoxically, however, Blumenberg himself does not succeed in grasping what the nature of Marx's greatness was. This is partly because the book is explicitly concerned with Marx's life and personality and only secondarily with his work. No study of Marx, however, can avoid assessing his political and intellectual achievement, and in this book the relationship between the man and his work is never satisfactorily resolved. Blumenberg's book was written at a time when a humanist and social-democratic interpretation of Marx and Marxism was at its height. This treatment of Marx and his work certainly marked a considerable advance on the Stalinist devotional tracts and vulgar bourgeois slanders which had passed for interpretations of Marx and Marxism in the 1940s and 1950s. But ultimately it does not represent an adequate assessment of Marx or of his real achievement. In Blumenberg's treatment, Marx emerges as a humanist philosopher: a thinker who discovered in the years 1843 and 1844 that the essence of man had become alienated in property relationships and that human freedom could only be realized in a classless socialist society; and a scholar who later buttressed his vision with an empirical economic foundation in *Capital.*

No account is taken of Marx's break with Hegel and Feuerbach, of his rupture with any form of epistemology based on a conception of human essence, and of his creation, together with Engels, of the completely new scientific terrain of historical materialism from 1845 onwards. Nor is any space devoted to Marx's momentous production of the concept of surplus value and his foundation of a Marxist economic science from around 1858. In Blumenberg's final analysis, Marx's importance today stems not from his creation of a new revolutionary theory, but from the grandeur of his humanism and the wealth of insights scattered throughout his works, which modern sociologists, historians and philosophers still find fruitful and thought-provoking.

Yet if we want to find reasons for Marx's lasting importance, it is upon his genius as the creator of a revolutionary and living science that we must insist. It is easy enough to discover from Marx's writings that he did not free himself at once from all reactionary sentiments – his utterances on women and national characteristics are a case in point.* What is astonishing is not that Marx should have possessed residues of conventional mid-Victorian prejudice, but rather the extent to which the

* It is necessary however to draw a distinction between Marx's positions in relation to these different phenomena. Marx's private utterances on sexuality, the family, child-rearing, the nature and place of women, etc. were undoubtedly in many respects in accord with the prevalent ideology of the time. On the other hand the question of interpreting Marx's formulations on race is different. In particular, Marx's alleged anti-semitism (to which Blumenberg alludes, pp. 6–8 and 52–4) cannot be understood except in the context of his hatred of all forms of national and ethnic particularism.

new science he founded opened the path to a theory capable of routing all such ideologies, even if he himself remained at times their victim. In as far as he was the creator of a scientific system, his personal failings or prejudices no more detract from it than Newton's devotion to Biblical commentaries disproves the validity of the law of gravity. Marx was both the founder of a science and a revolutionary militant. It is with the aid of the science inaugurated by him that we are able to analyse his lapses and misjudgements as a revolutionary. Marx was also, as Blumenberg shows more fully than ever before, a man with an often tragic private life, which under the circumstances of the time could never be wholly integrated with his practice as a political militant. Yet the nature of that life, haunted by poverty, disease and death was a direct consequence of Marx's unswerving loyalty to the struggle of the working class.

Gareth Stedman Jones

1

INTRODUCTION: THE PROBLEM OF A BIOGRAPHY

> Particularly in the case of Marx, most critics (whether hostile or friendly) have concentrated on the work rather than the author, on Marxism rather than on Marx. They have not seen clearly enough that both the transitory and the permanent elements in his passionately turbulent work can best be understood by considering the abilities, the historical background and the personal destiny of the man of flesh and blood.
>
> *Gustav Mayer*

The voluminous literature of the ideological dispute between East and West is one indication that Karl Marx does not belong to the past, but rather that his influence, even today, continues to be the strongest intellectual force of the nineteenth century. This is shown even more forcibly by the fact that there are whole areas in which 'Marxism' has become a dominant and influential ideology offering a constant potential alternative to other forms of state and society.

More than ninety per cent of the confusing and overwhelming wealth of literature about Marx is concerned with his theories, and it is by no means true to say that every book helps to clarify these theories or awakens interest in the reader. There is continual argument about Marx's theories, and in the process the creator of them is deliberately overlooked. But Marx was not a scholar striving to obtain 'objective' knowledge; he was (as Engels rightly said of him) 'more than half a revolutionary politician'. And therefore, since his theoretical work was openly intended to justify his political aims, it is hard to see why so little attention should be paid to the strong personality traits which were so important in the construction of this work.

Hence the epigraph by Gustav Mayer, which dates from 1918, is still absolutely valid today. Nor can we take as completely absurd the view of E.H. Carr, with which he prefaced his biography of Marx written in the thirties: that the Marxist assumption that Marxism had come directly from heaven like the Tables of the Law, or had sprung fully armed like Athene from the head of its creator, was completely unmarxist. For there is no reason to exclude Marxism from the Marxist law, which says that every idea is a product of the social conditions of the period in which it arose. Hence Marx's life must be important for an understanding of Marxism.

The classic biography of Marx is that by Franz Mehring, which also appeared in 1918; despite many other publications it has not been improved upon so far. Before and since, various biographies, large and small, have appeared which, depending on their attitude to Marx's ideas, have usually employed bright or sombre colours. Even the literature favourable to Marx is heavily interspersed with legend and prefers to adopt an apologetic tone. It is noteworthy that even Marx's supporters were always in a certain state of embarrassment with regard to him: Marx was really different from how he had been represented, and they knew this.

This astonishing fact is illustrated by Mehring's research itself. He was probably the person who was best acquainted with Marx the man. By far the most important source for a biography of Marx was his correspondence with Friedrich Engels, issued in 1913 after being seriously abridged by Bebel and Bernstein. All authorities as well as the leading socialists were agreed that drastic abbreviations were 'necessary', on both 'moral' and propagandistic grounds. It was *impermissible* for Marx to be as he disclosed himself. Marx, the discoverer of infallible objective laws operating with absolute certainty, must himself be entirely free from subjectivity, if he was to serve as a source of certainty. But now the correspondence with Engels showed that he was a person of the most extreme subjectivity, with the result that the very thing which constituted his greatness as a man was bound to impair the consistency of his views. In one of the reports he submitted, Mehring bluntly stated his opinion that, if this correspondence were to appear in full, all the efforts that he himself, Kautsky, Bernstein and others had been making for twenty years to preserve Marx's literary reputation would have been in vain. And although he recommended all future students of Marx to 'keep absolutely immune from all attacks of "Marxolatry"', we can see where his own better judgement led him to fob the reader off with not always very clear intimations.

To have published the Marx–Engels correspondence in full is one of the great services performed by David Riazanov, the founder and for many years the director of the Marx–Engels Institute in Moscow. This monumental work appeared from 1929 to 1931, in four solid volumes of the *Collected Edition* of Marx and Engels. Riazanov was justifiably convinced that Marx had the right to appear just as he really was; and that the world had the right to make the acquaintance of this great man as he actually was. But it was clear at once that Riazanov's great publication posed a number of problems to students of Marx which have still not been fully mastered even today. It was also clear that many accounts used as principal sources for portraying Marx's personality – such as those by his children or a number of his friends – had lost much of their value. These had not become completely useless; but now so much material of a different kind had to be set against them that Marx could no longer be viewed plainly and simply as a model citizen or hero, but was seen to be a very difficult and complicated personality.

Just as it was a great service to publish this correspondence, so it is a great pity that during the ensuing thirty years this rich material has not been used as the basis for a comprehensive and really accurate biography. The great work by Auguste Cornu has so far only reached the beginning of the forties, still a fairly neutral period. On the other hand the correspondence was responsible for the distorted picture that Leopold Schwarzschild drew of Marx. Werner Sombart, after his panegyric in *Das Lebenswerk von Karl Marx* (published in 1909), justified his change of heart about Marx by saying that the correspondence (which he only knew in the abridged edition) was 'nauseating' and showed 'what a thoroughly corroded soul had dwelt in Marx'. Marx's *misère* did not give him a better opinion of the man, but only shocked him; and later, of course, Sombart went much further. The same applies to Schwarzschild. It is astonishing that this eminent publicist, who produced one of the best German periodicals (with his *Tagebuch* during the Weimar Period, and his *Neues Tagebuch* during the emigration), could adopt the amazing opinion that a man was the sum of his mistakes, or that a work such as Marx's, with its immense scale and its world-wide application, could be explained in terms of weaknesses of character. However his view was not entirely accidental: he wished to reveal Marx as the origin of all totalitarian states, and wanted to forge a weapon for the Cold War. Even today it is possible for a French scholar, Maximilien Rubel, to speak of '*Marx cet inconnu*'. And a great deal of detailed work is necessary before we can say that we possess a picture of Marx that does him justice.

2

ANCESTORS, FAMILY LIFE AND SCHOOL

Karl Heinrich Marx was born on 5 May 1818 in Trier, then a small country town of twelve thousand inhabitants. His father, Heinrich Marx, was a lawyer, whose marriage with Henriette Pressburg had been blessed with four sons and five daughters. The eldest son, Moritz-David, died in 1818, soon after he was born. In Marx's life we shall later encounter the elder sister Sophie, as the wife of the advocate Schmalhausen in Maastricht, and also the two younger sisters: Louise, who married the law student Juta and emigrated to South Africa, and Emilie, wife of the engineer Conradi in Trier. During the time that Marx spent in his parents' house, up to 1836, four others – Hermann, Henriette, Karoline and Eduard – were still alive. They all died young from tuberculosis. In this large family Karl Marx spent a happy childhood. Family life was harmonious, and relations with the parents were affectionate; among their circle of acquaintances there reigned the sentimental atmosphere of the Biedermeier period. The family enjoyed a certain middle-class prosperity. The father acquired some standing in his profession, became a magistrate, and in 1819 was able to afford his own house, No. 8 Simeonstrasse, close by the Porta Nigra, into which the family moved from the house at No. 10 Brückenstrasse, the 'Karl Marx House'.

The forebears of the father as well as the mother had been rabbis for many generations; it was an old custom that the children of rabbis tended to intermarry. Genealogical researches have given us some information about the family tree.* Jewish scholars have rightly objected that

---

* B. Wachstein, 'Die Abstammung von Karl Marx' in *Festskrift i anledng af Professor David Simonsens 70-aarige fødseldag* (Copenhagen, 1923), 277 ff.; E. Lewin-Dorsch, 'Familie und Stammbaum von Karl Marx' in *Die Glocke* (Berlin, 1923), IX, 1, 309 ff. and 340 ff.; H. Horowitz, 'Die Familie Lwow' in *Monatsschrift für Geschichte und Wissenschaft des Judentums* (Frankfurt, 1928), 72, 487 ff.

The house in Trier where Marx was born

biographies of Marx have paid little attention to this family tradition. Thus Eugen Lewin-Dorsch says the following about Mehring's treatment in his big biography:

> In his book of more than 500 pages ... this great expert and exponent of Prussian history has clearly not been able to interest himself greatly in this aspect of his biography of Marx. But we cannot help agreeing with Oncken when (in his biography of Lassalle) he says: 'In a man's biography the

> period of growth is always more fruitful and attractive than the period of achievement.' Although – or perhaps precisely because – Marx almost deliberately overlooked his Jewish descent, it falls to his biographer to trace the threads that bind him to the Jewish world. And first we must pay attention to the rabbinical element.... Of course one must certainly not exaggerate the emphasis on such a background, but on the other hand one must not dismiss it too lightly. For instance Mehring says that Marx's father had already 'completely outgrown his Jewishness', that the son 'had taken over this complete freedom from all Jewish prejudice as a valuable gift from his parental home', and that in the letters he received from his father 'there were no traces, either good or bad, of Jewishness'. Such an evasive and at the same time disparaging and ignorant verdict on the matter is of little use. It merely touches the superficies of intellectual life, the individual's consciousness of self; it does not penetrate to the depths, where the forces of personality are mysteriously and invisibly formed. Marx himself has said, 'The tradition of all past generations weighs like a mountain on the minds of the living.' And if we wish to understand the full humanity of this man, we must also take into account this inheritance from his rabbinical past, the importance of which he himself certainly never fully realized. The enlightened culture of his parental home, his father's conversion to Protestantism, even his own strong and steadily emphasized antipathy towards the Jewish commercial spirit cannot really outweigh the 'tradition of all past generations' which was present in him too.

Marx's father was born in Saarlautern in 1782, the third son of the Rabbi Meier Halevi Marx. The latter subsequently became the rabbi in Trier, and he was followed in this office by his eldest son Samuel, who died in 1827. There were a number of rabbis among his ancestors. In the family of the wife of Meier Halevi Marx we find many important scholars. This wife, the grandmother of Karl Marx, was Chaje, the daughter of Moses Lwow, who had also been a rabbi in Trier. And the latter's father, Josua Heschel Lwow, was Rabbi of Trier in 1723, and Rabbi of Ansbach after 1733. He was a great scholar; and it was said of him that no decision was ever taken in the Jewish world without his opinion first being sought. His father in turn was Aron Lwow, who in his youth had also been the Rabbi in Trier and after about 1693 was Rabbi of Westhofen in Alsace. He was a son of the scholar Moses Lwow of Lemberg. Amongst his ancestors there were famous men such as the Cracow scholar Josef ben Gerson ha-Cohen, Meir Katzenellenbogen, rabbi and head of the talmudic college in Padua (d. 1565), and Abraham ha-Levi Minz (i.e. from Mainz, died about 1525) Rabbi of Padua. The latter's father (born about 1408) had left Germany about the middle of the century on account of the persecutions and was 'one of the greatest authorities of the German and Italian Jewish communities'.

Trier in the early nineteenth century

Marx's grandfather on his mother's side or one of his ancestors had emigrated from Hungary to Holland; this grandfather was Rabbi of Nijmegen. A sister of the mother, Sophie, married the banker Lion Philips, grandfather of the founder of the Philips business. Marx often visited this family in Zaltbommel; he frequently had financial dealings with the uncle, who acted as trustee for his mother, and until 1870 he was certainly friendly with these Dutch relatives.

During the Middle Ages (which in the case of the Jews lasted until about 1800) the Jewish communities possessed full autonomy in their own affairs. From an economic, religious and cultural point of view, the communities carried on an independent life; as far as the state and city were concerned, they were represented principally by their rabbis. Since the communities largely had their own legislation and jurisdiction for civil rights, the rabbi was also directly concerned in looking after these; it was to him, and not to the secular court, that the Jews would appeal when they were in difficulties. The rabbi was not so much concerned with preaching and the cure of souls; he was first and foremost a teacher and a scholar. During the post-talmudic period the Jewish laws were no longer codified; judgement was given on the basis of the Talmud, while in difficult cases this was done after written opinions had been invited from well-known scholars. These opinions were founded on detailed exegesis according to established patterns. A glance at the literature concerned with these patterns – hermeneutic induction, analogy, antinomy or syllogism – gives some idea of this method, making the fullest possible use of exegesis, extremely subtle and frequently leading to sophistries. At any event the delivering of these opinions presupposed a comprehensive knowledge of the tradition, the Halacha of the Talmud, a knowledge that could only be acquired by unremitting study. In the family tree we are concerned with several men who were renowned in the literature of these opinions, men such as Joshua Heschel Lwow and Josef ben Gerson Ha-Cohen. If we visualize the character of the early rabbihood, we may say that Karl Marx represented both the summit and the product of a century-old tradition of scholars.

There is many a trait in his personality that one is tempted to ascribe to particular ancestors, for example his combativeness to that same Joshua Heschel Lwow. On occasions it has happened that these influences have been summarily passed over, as for instance when Arthur Sakheim called him 'the exegetist and talmudist of sociology'. Marx's astonishing gift for association, the acuteness of his thought, his power of exposition, the subtlety of his polemics and his mastery of dialectic have all been seen as the heritage of this long line of scholars trained in intellectual work and sharpness of understanding. Georg Adler emphasizes the 'natural responsiveness of Marx's mind' to radical deduction, and his 'tendency towards abstraction, deduction and construction', which must have been even more strongly developed by his study of the philosophy of Hegel. However this may be, one must by no means overlook Marx's ancestors. Such is the view of all Jewish scholars, and hence of those best able to gauge possible influences (for example, Adler, Dubnow, Farbstein, Horowitz, Lewin-Dorsch, Mayer, Sakheim, Wachstein and de Wolff). Many researchers link Marx up with the old prophets. But this, like Marx's alleged antisemitism, is something we shall have more to say about later.

At the age of thirty-five, in the year 1816 or 1817, Marx's father had himself baptized; but instead of joining the Catholic faith, which was predominant in Trier, he adopted the evangelical creed. He chose the latter because, like Heine, he equated Protestantism with intellectual freedom. Whereas in Poland the education of Jews consisted solely of Hebraic and rabbinical studies, and anything outside this sphere counted as being hostile to religion (for example, Moses Mendelssohn's attempt to translate the Pentateuch into German met with a religious ban), in Western Germany the spirit of the Enlightenment had to some extent

Marx's birth certificate

penetrated into evangelical and Catholic, as well as Jewish, circles. It was no accident that Börne, Heine, Hess and Marx all came from the Rhineland. Even Heinrich Marx had read Voltaire, Rousseau and Kant and emancipated himself from the beliefs of the synagogue; he cultivated deist views and recommended to his son 'the pure belief in God' such as one found in Locke, Newton and Leibniz and which was such an effective support for morality. But for him baptism was not, as it had been for Heine, merely the 'entrance-ticket to European culture'. It was not even necessitated by persecution of the Jews in the Rhineland and in Alsace at this time. A much more direct occasion for it was the situation of constraint created for the Jews by the reaction after the fall of Napoleon. In Prussia in 1815 they were excluded from all public offices, and by a decision of the Minister of the Interior on 4 May 1816 the definition of public office was extended to include legal practice and the carrying on of a chemist's shop. Even a recommendation by the president of the Commission for Summary Justice, that (on account of his outstanding qualifications) Heinrich Marx should be accepted into the judicial service, was rejected by the Minister. Thus if he wanted to continue in his profession, which he had worked hard to enter despite privations and domestic conflicts, he would have to undergo baptism. This step meant a complete break with his family. His brother Samuel died in 1827 as the senior rabbi of Trier, and after that his sister-in-law and other relatives lived in the town. Naturally the families knew each other; but nothing is known of any close bond between them. Nor is it known whether Heinrich Marx spoke to his son at the time about the reasons for his baptism.

The children were baptized on 26 August 1824, but the mother not until 20 November 1825; she delayed this step out of respect for her father who was still alive. The pressure that forced Heinrich Marx to move over to Christianity tended to strengthen his liberal and oppositional inclinations. These were expressed in January 1834 at the social club, on the occasion of a banquet in honour of the Trier deputies to the Rhine Landtag. In his speech Justizrat Marx made mention of the King, 'to whose magnanimity we owe the first steps towards national representation. In the fullness of his omnipotence he has, of his own free will, instituted assemblies of the estates, in order that truth should advance to the steps of his throne' . Although the King had repeatedly broken his solemn promises to allow a constitution, there was absolutely no irony intended in this remark; but the government viewed this banquet – one of many similar events that took place at this time under the slogan of a constitution – as being an expression of the liberal spirit. And soon afterwards there were great goings-on at the commemoration banquet of the social club. There was a singing of the 'Marseillaise', of 'Was ist des Deutschen Vaterland?', and other 'infamous songs'. Even Marx's father, denounced by certain officers, was involved in the subsequent investigation, and henceforth the government regarded him as one of those 'from whom no sort of conciliation was to be expected in the present tension between Prussia and the Rhineland'. Karl Marx was then sixteen years old.

At the same time the liberalism of the father was very moderate. He was altogether loyal and much too mild for his opposition to be really determined. His attitude towards Prussia was patriotic, in contrast to the anti-Prussian feeling that was predominant in Trier. When his student son was planning to write poetry, he recommended him to take, as the subject for 'an ode on the grand scale', some episode from Prussian history, for example the Battle of Waterloo, which would do honour to Prussia and would allow 'the Genius of the Monarchy … to play a role'. A poem of this kind would also help his son's career.

For five years Karl Marx went to the Jesuit school in Trier, which during the Prussian period was known as the Friedrich-Wilhelm Gymnasium. The school had a good reputation, chiefly owing to the fact that it was run by the Principal Wyttenbach who was very much respected by the people of the Rhineland as a Kantian and a liberal, although the authorities did not approve of him so much. He taught Marx history. In his leaving-certificate the candidate showed good marks in the classics, in German and in history, but was less industrious in mathematics and in French. His German essay was described as being 'really good', though the author fell 'into his usual mistake here of exaggeratedly struggling to find the unusual and ornate epithet'. It was stated that he could translate the Latin and Greek classics with care and proficiency, even the more difficult passages, 'especially those where the difficulty was not so much in the oddity of the language as in the matter itself and the connection of the ideas'. His knowledge of French was good, and also of religious doctrine and mathematics; he was fairly skilled in history and geography; on the other hand his knowledge of physics was only moderate.

From the candidate's religious essay, in which he was asked to show 'How the believer is joined with Christ according to John XIV, with all its necessity and consequences', attempts have been made to deduce a basic Christian attitude for Marx. But this is incorrect. The youth, who was baptized without being asked, could say nothing about religious experience. As far as he was concerned, religion meant ethics: it was only through Christ that man had become capable of a pure Christian virtue, something which 'the peoples of antiquity, the heathen', could not achieve. Hence there was a need for union with Christ, which could give 'an inner elevation, comfort in sorrow, calm trust and a heart susceptible to human love, to everything noble and great, not for the sake of ambition or glory, but only for the sake of Christ'. This must not be seen as a creed; soon Marx was to reject Christianity as firmly as Judaism.

Much more important than this formal exercise is his German essay, 'Considerations of a Young Man on Choosing his Career'. The seventeen-year-old sees man's vocation not in the attainment of a brilliant social position that will satisfy his ambition, but in striving for fulfilment and working for humanity. Guided by this, the young man should choose his calling to correspond with his capabilities. But his choice could never be quite free; for

> to some extent we have already acquired relationships in society before we are in a position to decide them. [We should choose the position] which

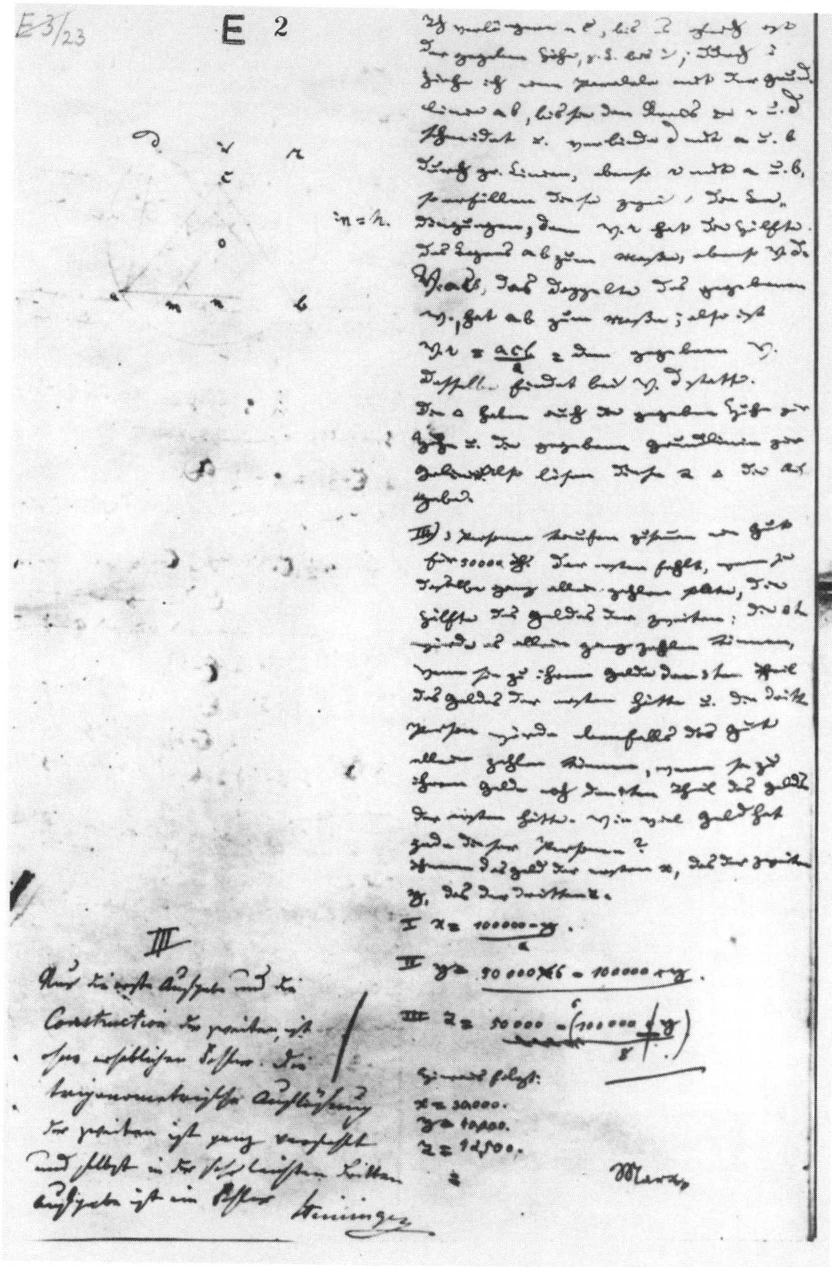

A page from Marx's *Abitur*

> affords us the greatest honour, which is founded on ideas that we thoroughly believe in, which offers us the greatest chance of working for humanity and of drawing near to that universal goal for which any position is only a stepping-stone, namely self-fulfilment.... Those positions which are not concerned with life so much as with abstract truths are the most dangerous for a young man.... If he is working only for himself he can become a famous scholar, a very wise man, or an eminent writer, but never a complete and truly great man. According to History the greatest men are those that have worked for the general good and ennobled themselves. Experience calls him the happiest who has made most people happy. Religion itself teaches us that the Ideal towards which all strive sacrificed Himself for humanity, and who shall dare to contradict such claims? If we have chosen the position in which we can accomplish the most for humanity, then we can never be crushed by the burdens because these are only sacrifices made for the sake of all. Then it is no poor, restricted, egoistic joy that we savour; on the contrary our happiness belongs to millions, our deeds live on calmly with endless effect, and our ashes will be moistened by the ardent tears of noble men.

This is the pure idealism of a young man who formulates his conception of life and his vocation in a rapturous and solemn manner; it was later to have a tacit effect in the life-work of the man, in the form of an enthusiasm for social ethics.

Little is known of Marx's relations with his schoolfellows. For the most part they were the sons of artisans and peasants, about half of whom chose a religious calling. Marx must have been popular with them, since he joined in their rambles, but he must also have been feared for his sarcasm. Later on he only once mentioned a schoolfellow, who had become known as an officer; but he mistook him for his cousin. If he struck up friendships, they can only have been the usual school friendships that do not generally last long. There was one schoolfellow with whom he kept up a friendship, but this was only because he became Marx's brother-in-law – Edgar von Westphalen, the brother of his future wife Jenny. He was a good-natured, weak man, who gave up his studies and followed Marx to Brussels where he subscribed to certain Communist resolutions. Twice he emigrated to Texas, lost everything, and finally he died in the eighties as a small legal official in Berlin. When he came home in 1865, he spent six months with the Marx family in London. At that time Frau Marx wrote about him to Frau Liebknecht: 'He was the idol of my childhood and when I was young, my sole beloved companion. I clung to him with all my heart.... In recent times I have had so often to deal with Karl's family, who treat me in a distant and alien fashion, that I hold fast all the more closely to this single link that is left to me of my own family.'

Judging by his achievements at school, Marx was just about average in his class. Doubtless his education owed more to his environment and his leisure activities than to the teaching. And by environment I mean principally his father and his future father-in-law, the Privy Councillor Ludwig von Westphalen. For the ripening maturity of the young man it was of the greatest importance, not only that these two men took him seriously, but that they were real friends to him. It is recounted that his father read French classics with him, and Westphalen read Greek poets and Shakespeare, and did so to such effect that Marx retained his enthusiasm for these writers all his life. Westphalen belonged to the Prussian administration, and no doubt he also spoke to his young friend about public affairs. We may assume that this was in a progressive spirit, since Westphalen also introduced him to Saint-Simon. Marx thanked him in the dedication to his Dissertation:

> My dear fatherly friend, you will forgive me if I dedicate an insignificant pamphlet to your dear name. I am too impatient to await another opportunity to give you some small token of my affection. Would that all could be as happy as I in admiring an old man with the force of youth, who greets every advance of progress with the enthusiasm and soberness of truth, and with that convincing shining idealism that is the sole source of truth; one to whom all minds in the world are clear, who never trembled at the shadows of reactionary ghosts or before the gloomy clouds of time, but with divine energy and manly gaze saw through all pupations into the very empyrean that burns in the heart of the world. You, my fatherly friend, have always been a living *argumentum ad oculos* that idealism was no mere illusion, but the truth.

It is the current view that Marx's father had very little understanding for him, and his mother none at all. As far as his father was concerned this view is entirely false. His correspondence with his son while at the university gives us some very important clues about Marx's youthful development. The mother was not very well educated, but she was a woman with very warm feelings who was entirely absorbed in looking after the family. The son could expect no intellectual stimulation from her. But she cherished a special love for him, although she really always had to be looking after her sick children. In her eyes, as in those of the father, Karl was 'the lucky one', much more gifted than his brothers and sisters, and she looked on him with great pride. The parents praise his clear understanding, the purity of his feelings, his sincerity and the openness and honesty of his character. When he was a student his mother sent him lots of good advice, although it gave her a great deal of trouble to write in German. For example, in November 1835:

> ... you must not think it merely a weakness of our sex if I am curious to hear how you have established your tiny household, and whether economy takes first place in it as it must in all households large and small, and here I must say dear Carl that you should never look upon cleanliness and order as a trivial matter since your health and spirits depend on it, make sure that your rooms are scrubbed out often, keep a regular time for it – and wash yourself every week my dear Carl with soap and sponge – how do you manage with coffee do you make it yourself or what, I beg you to tell me everything to do with housekeeping, I only hope your beloved muse will not feel insulted by your mother's prose for I can tell you that humble things help one to attain the highest and best, now if you wish for anything at Christmas that I can give you then I shall be happy to do it, so goodbye my dear dear Carl, be a good boy, think always of God and your parents, your loving mother Henriette Marx. All the children send their love and kisses and as always you are the best and most beloved.*

The son speaks of his mother as *Mütterchen* and 'Angel-Mother'. But he had no real inner bond with her. Immediately after the death of his father even the formal link with his family was broken. As far as his brothers and sisters were concerned, Marx seems to have had a close relationship for a time only with his eldest sister Sophie. She was a friend of Jenny von Westphalen and thus remained intimate with her and with her brother.

* *Translator's note*: I have followed the lack of punctuation in the original.

3

LIFE AT THE UNIVERSITY – CONFLICT WITH HIS FATHER

Marx was at university from October 1835 until March 1841, at Bonn and Berlin; he spent two semesters at the former, and nine at the latter. At the wish of his father he studied law, although his father had not required him to practise it. Later on Marx himself described jurisprudence as being his subject; but in fact he only studied it as a subordinate subject to philosophy and history. In practice, lectures in law began to figure less and less in his studies, while their place was now filled by philosophy and history. In Bonn, besides attending the regular law course, he gave himself a taste of the humanities with 'Mythology of the Greeks and Romans', as well as modern art history and August Wilhelm von Schlegel on 'Questions about Homer' and 'The Elegies of Propertius'. Again in Berlin the first semesters were largely taken up with jurisprudence. In addition to Savigny on 'Pandects' he chiefly went to hear lectures on criminal law and Prussian provincial law, given by the liberal Hegelian, Eduard Gans. Of philosophical lectures he heard only one on logic given by the dry Hegelian, Gabler; but he also attended lectures on anthropology and geography. During two semesters he put his name down for no lectures; in one he attended only a course of lectures on Isaiah by his friend Bruno Bauer, and in the other he went to only one lecture on Euripides. As regards the lectures by Gans and the one on logic he is reported to have shown great industry; in the case of the former he was attracted chiefly by the lecturer, who also dealt with contemporary questions, and in the latter by the subject. Since no lists have been preserved we do not know which other lectures were of interest to Marx.

One thing that is certain is that in the field of his own subjects, philosophy and history, he largely went his own way. This is clear from

The Trier student club in Bonn (Marx marked with ×)

a series of student-notebooks for the years 1840-41, which contain extracts from the works of Aristotle, Spinoza, Leibniz, Hume, and notes on the history of Kantian philosophy. It is conspicuous that a part of these extracts made on the reading, as well as the Dissertation, are not in the hand of Marx himself but have been written by a copyist. There are no indications of an intensive study of Hegel, such as was encouraged in the circle of the Young Hegelians. It is interesting to note that Aristotle is studied in connection with Hegel and his dialectic is developed:

> If Aristotle takes synthesis to be the basis of all error, this is entirely correct. Reflective thought is in all respects a synthesis of being and thinking, of the universal and the particular, of appearances and reality. So then all incorrect thinking, including incorrect perception, conscious-

The young Marx (enlargement from previous picture)

> ness, etc., consists of syntheses of such determinations as do not belong together; it does not consist of immanent relationships between objective and subjective determinations.

Marx took an enthusiastic part in student life. He belonged to the Trier group (student corps were forbidden) and even became one of their presidents. He was imprisoned for drunkenness and for disturbing the peace, and was accused of carrying prohibited weapons. Once he even took part in a duel. In the certificate he received on graduating from Berlin it was noted that he had several times been accused of debts, but that he had been acquitted of participating in a prohibited association among the students.

We are much better informed about Marx's literary efforts, which may have given him some claim to merit in Bonn and during the first year in Berlin. In Bonn he belonged to a poetry circle of which Emanuel Geibel was also a member. For a long time Marx was seriously occupied with literary plans. He was even thinking of founding a periodical for dramatic criticism, and he sent poems to Adalbert von Chamisso for his *Musenalmanach*. Although the young poet soon repudiated his productions, two 'Savage Poems' were considered worthy of publication in the *Athenäum*. He assembled his pieces into three notebooks of poems and songs which he sent to his betrothed, and one book entitled *Poems* which his father received on his birthday: romances and ballads, one act of a hair-raising tragedy in verse, and several chapters of a comic novel in which philistinism is satirized in the manner of Laurence Sterne and E.T.A. Hoffmann. As early as 1839 he had made a collection for his betrothed of folk songs from various sources. All these efforts are on a considerable scale, and for a long time Marx wavered between philosophy and poetry, returning continually to his earlier productions. Later on he laughed at these verses as youthful follies; and ever since Mehring declared them to be valueless, every critic has agreed with this view. Hence they are only of biographical interest. They lack technical form and show an exaggerated expression of will and feeling, and in presenting the individual problems of a young man: melancholy, longing, love, disappointment. One poem runs:

Never can I calmly practise
that which strongly grips my soul,
Never can I rest in comfort
And I rage unceasingly

For I wish to win all prizes,
Every favour of the Gods,
Daringly press on in knowledge
And embrace all art and song.

Therefore let us venture all things,
Never resting, never stopping,
But eschew a gloomy silence
Or a lack of wish and deed.

Nor descend in anxious brooding
To that other humble yoke,
For the power to wish and clamour
And to act, is with us still.

Apart from philosophical aphorisms there are a large number of ballads and romances, in which the usual themes of romantic literature are dealt with and all the familiar requisites of romantic poetry appear: an enchanted harp, nostalgia, love of the night, the song of the sirens, the singing harp-girl, the pale maiden, the magic boat, the man in the moon, a dream-picture, night thoughts, and so forth. At this time Marx also seems to have kept a journal, and during the Biedermeier period the usual reason for this was not in order to fill it with one's abundant emotional life, but in order to let those close to one share in it. Thus he occasionally imparted some of it to his father. As for his novel, he himself considered the humour was 'forced'; and we shall be quite ready to believe that he lacked a sense of humour when we read his great letter of confession to his father.

This curious report, the only letter we know Marx to have written to his parents, tells us something about his inner development; it was occasioned by serious disagreements with his father, who was watching his son's development with growing anxiety. For Marx, the relationship with his father was of the greatest importance. Apart from four letters from his mother and his sister Sophie, the only family letters he kept were the seventeen letters from his father; and it is said that for the rest of his life Marx always carried a photograph of his father, which Engels put into his coffin with him. In the way his relationship with his father developed we see a reflection of the development of the young Marx's personality. If we rely to a large extent on the letters of the father, it is because they provide a mirror of particular clarity; for the father took a special interest in all Karl's affairs, and he possessed a quite extraordinary understanding for his difficult and highly gifted son.

The elder Marx expected much of his son and made great demands on him: 'I should like to see in you what I myself perhaps might have become, if I had seen the light under such favourable auspices. It is in your hands to fulfil or to destroy my greatest hopes.' But he makes no excessive demands, and does not spur his son on to work harder; on the contrary he is afraid that he may overtax himself: 'Don't wear yourself out. You've got time enough, please God, to live for the good of yourself and your family, and also (if I divine correctly) for the good of humanity.' He begs him to look after his health, 'there is no more pitiable being than a sickly scholar'.

He is just as reluctant to stipulate any particular career for his son; this is remarkable in that time of patriarchal authority, when a career in a middle-class profession was usually laid down at the beginning of a course of study. When after two semesters the son begins thinking of an academic teaching post, the father takes a serious interest. But he leaves his son completely free about this; there is not even any question of the faculty, although the son is studying law. Even philosophy seems quite acceptable to the father, and much more suitable to the son.

The father is just as understanding about his son's literary plans, although he is quite baffled by several productions: '...*à propos*! I have read your poem carefully. I confess to you frankly, my dear Karl, I don't understand it – either the real meaning or the general drift.... Do you delight only in abstract ideal notions (just about equivalent to nonsense)? In short, tell me the answer, I confess my limitations.' He altogether agrees with his son that the poems should not be printed immediately; a poet or writer should be able to offer something powerful if he wishes to appear before the public. 'I tell you frankly, I am really pleased with your abilities and I expect much from them, but I should be sorry to see you turn out to be an ordinary sort of little poet.... One has to be outstanding before one has the right to claim the attention of the jaded public.' The father discusses with his son in detail the plan for founding a magazine of theatrical criticism. He thinks it will be very difficult to win the confidence of a good bookseller: 'If you succeed in this – and you have always been a lucky one – then comes a second [question]. Either philosophy or law or both of them together would seem excellent as a foundation. Genuine poetry can well take second place, and will never injure the reputation, unless in the eyes of certain pedants,' and the father does not count himself one of these. When Karl had been in Bonn three weeks and had not yet written, his father accused him of 'infinite laziness': 'Unfortunately I find that this confirms only too well my opinion that, in spite of your many good qualities, there is a predominant egoism in your personality.' But after his son has written back, he hastens to confess that he is wrong and gives the anxiety of the mother as the reason for the reproach. He is convinced of his son's good qualities. He begs that his son will always remain as sincere and frank, and will look upon his parents as his best friends. In many small matters he gives him good advice. The son ought not to neglect social connections that might be useful to him; and he himself takes some trouble to procure such introductions. With reference to the teaching post, he recommends his son to train his voice a little; for Marx always retained certain traces of the Rhineland dialect. He also implores him to write more legibly.

Then came a conflict which only ended with the death of the father: in autumn 1836 Karl became secretly engaged to Jenny von Westphalen,

Jenny von Westphalen

who was four years older than him. The father was frightened that his son might place himself in an equivocal position with Jenny's very respectable family, especially as the girl was much courted; and he himself had so much respect for that family that the ambiguous relationship was a heavy burden to him. So his demands to his son became more urgent:

> A man has no more sacred duty than that which he assumes towards a weaker woman.... But if after serious self-examination you really persist in this view, then you must become a man at once.... You have taken on important duties, and my dear Karl, at the risk of offending you, I must speak my mind in my own somewhat prosaic fashion. With all the exaggerations and exaltations of love in a poetic mind you will not be able to secure the tranquillity of the being, to whom you must devote yourself entirely; on the contrary, you run the danger of destroying this tranquillity.... She brings you an inestimable treasure – she demonstrates a self-denial which only the coldest reason can fully estimate. Woe to you if you do not remember this for the rest of your life! But now at least you must act for yourself. You yourself must provide the certainty that, in spite of your youth, you are a man who deserves the respect of the world.... I beg and implore you, now that you really possess this treasure, although everything is not yet smooth, to moderate these storms of passion, and take care not to stir them up in the breast of this being who deserves and requires calm.... You know, my dear Karl, that for love of you I have agreed to something that is not really in keeping with my character and from time

to time it certainly gives me anxiety.... I cannot and will not conceal my weakness towards you. Sometimes my heart revels in thoughts of you and your future. And yet sometimes I cannot drive away sad, ominous, fearful ideas when the thought suddenly creeps in: does your heart match your head and your abilities? Does your heart really have room for the earthly but gentler feelings, which are so very comforting to Man in this Vale of Sorrows? And, since your heart is clearly enlivened and governed by a spirit that is not given to all men, I ask whether this spirit is of a heavenly or a Faustian nature? Do you think – and this is not the least painful of my doubts – that you will ever be capable of feeling a truly human, a domestic happiness? ... You will ask what has put these ideas into my head. Well I have often had similar fantastic ideas, and I could easily chase them away, for I have always had a great need to give you all the love and respect I was capable of, and I am glad not to think of myself. But I see a striking phenomenon in Jenny. She occasionally shows involuntarily a kind of fear, a fear full of foreboding, which I cannot help noticing.... What can this be? I cannot explain it, but unhappily my own experience will not allow me to be easily misled about it. Your advancement in the world, the flattering hope of eventually seeing your name highly renowned, as well as your happiness on earth, are all close to my heart, they are illusions I have long fostered.... But I can assure you that the realisation of these illusions would not be enough to make me happy. Only if your heart remains pure and beats like a man's, only if no demonic spirit has the power to alienate your heart from better feelings – only then shall I find the happiness that for years I have been dreaming I might find through you; else I should see the finest goal of my life destroyed. Yet why do I indulge myself and perhaps sadden you? Really I have no doubt of your love towards me and your dear mother, and you know very well where we are most vulnerable.... Perhaps it is a very good and salutary thing that immediately on entering the world you are forced to show consideration for others, yes, even wisdom, foresight and mature reflection, in spite of any demons....

This letter hit the son very hard. He became impatient because his fiancée refused to write before the engagement was announced. His father appealed to his manliness and rebuked him:

I leave you to judge for yourself whether I was right to get angry. You know very well, you *must* know, the love I have for you. Your letters (insofar as they are not merely sickly sentimentality and gloomy imaginings) show need enough.... Although I love you more than anything – with the exception of your mother – I am not blind, and I wish to be even less so. I give you your due entirely, but I cannot quite get rid of the idea that you are not free from egoism, that you have more of it than one needs for self-preservation.... Don't throw the blame on your character. It's no use accusing Nature, she has certainly treated you like a mother. She has given you enough strength, and will-power depends on the man. But to yield to pain at the smallest difficulty, to lay your heart bare at every sorrow and to tear apart our love for you, do you call that poetry? ... No, it is only weakness, pampering, egotism and conceit that reduce everything to self in that way and thrust

> one's dearest ones into the background! ... But for your own sake I shall never stop lecturing you until I am convinced that this blemish has gone from your otherwise noble character....

It was perhaps too much to expect that at nineteen years of age one should be full of worldly wisdom; but if at this age one was going to bind to oneself the fate of a young girl, then one must have a sober grasp of 'the real meaning of life'. The father's remarks do not show any anger at the course adopted by his son; but they do show a growing anger that the son is entering into bourgeois obligations without troubling himself about how these obligations can be fulfilled. Finally he asks for a concise review of his son's 'positive studies in law'. When the son does not comply, but instead sends a 'piece of writing without form or content, an incoherent uninformative fragment', the father reprimands him seriously :

> Your previous letter had said much to arouse my expectations. I had written several times asking for detailed information. And instead of that I get a disjointed and incoherent and (which is even worse) a *confused* letter. To be frank with you, my dear Karl, I do not like that modern word, which is one that all weaklings hide behind when they get angry with the world because it does not give them splendid palaces and carriages and untold millions without them having to do any work or have any trouble. I find this confusedness revolting, and you were the last person I expected it from. What reason can you have for it? Has not everything smiled on you since the day you were born? Has Nature not showered gifts on you? Have your parents not squandered love on you? Have you ever lacked anything to satisfy any wish within reason? And have you not won in a marvellous fashion the love of a young woman, whom thousands envy you? And yet the first sign of opposition, the first disappointed wish, brings out all this confusion! Is that what you call strength? Is that a manly character?

This letter crossed with Marx's great confessional letter of 10 November 1837, which certainly gave a review of his 'positive studies', but otherwise confirmed all his father's fears regarding the future:

> Dear Father,
>
> There are moments in one's life that represent the limit of a period and at the same time point clearly in a new direction....
>
> So now that I am casting an eye back over the events of the year that I have lived here, and thus answering, my dear Father, your most precious letter from Ems, allow me to consider my situation (as I do life in general) as the result of an intellectual activity that finds expression on all sides – in science, art and personal matters.
>
> When I left you, a new world had just begun to exist for me, a world of love that was at first drunk with its own desire and hopeless. Even the journey to Berlin which would otherwise have charmed me completely,

1a Alte Leipziger Strasse, where Marx first lived in Berlin

excited me to an admiration of nature and inflamed me with a zest for life, left me cold and even, surprisingly, depressed me; for the rocks that I saw were not rougher, not harsher than the emotions of my soul, the broad cities not more full of life than my blood, the tables of the inns not more overladen and indigestible than the stocks of fantasies that I carried with me, nor, finally, was any work of art as beautiful as Jenny.

When I arrived in Berlin I broke off all the relations that I had hitherto contracted, made rare and reluctant visits and tried to steep myself in science and art.

Considering my state of mind then it was inevitable that lyric poetry should be my first project and certainly the pleasantest and readiest to hand. But my attitude and all my previous development made it purely idealistic....

But poetry was to be, and had to be, only a sideline; I had to study jurisprudence and felt above all impelled to struggle with philosophy. Both were so interconnected that I examined Heineccius, Thibaut and the sources completely uncritically like a schoolboy and thus translated the first two books of Pandects into German and at the same time tried to elaborate a philosophy that would cover the whole field of law. As introduction I prefixed a few metaphysical propositions and continued this unhappy opus as far as public law, a work of almost three hundred pages....

But why should I go on filling up pages with what I have rejected? The whole is full of hair-splitting, it is written with boring prolixity and Roman conceptions are barbarously misused in order to force them into my system. On the other hand, this did give me, at least to some extent, a love and knowledge of the material.

At the end of material private law I saw the falsity of the whole conception (whose outline borders on the Kantian but when elaborated veers completely away), and it again became plain to me that I could not get by without philosophy. So I was forced again with a quiet conscience to throw myself into her arms and composed a new basic system of metaphysics at the end of which I was forced to realize the perversity of this, and that of all my previous efforts....

At the end of the term I again sought the dances of the Muses and the music of the Satyrs.... And yet these last poems were the only ones in which suddenly, as though at the touch of a magic wand – oh! the touch was at first shattering – the kingdom of true poetry glittered opposite me like a distant fairy palace and all my creations dissolved into nothingness.

With these various occupations I had been forced during the first term to sit up through many nights, to fight through many a struggle and endure much excitement from within and without, and yet was not much richer at the end in spite of having deserted nature, art and the world, and spurned friends. These thoughts were registered by my body and a doctor advised me to go to the country, and so for the first time I went through the whole length of the city and out of the gate to Stralow. I did not suspect that there my anaemic and languishing body would mature and acquire a robust strength.

A curtain had fallen, my Holy of Holies was rent asunder and new gods had to be installed. I left behind the idealism which, by the way, I had nourished with that of Kant and Fichte, and came to seek the idea in the real itself. If the gods had before dwelt above the earth, they had now become its centre.

I had read fragments of Hegel's philosophy, but I did not care for its grotesque and rocky melody. Once again I wanted to dive off into the sea, but with the firm intention of finding the nature of the mind as necessary, concrete and firmly established as that of physical nature, for I wanted to stop fencing and bring the pure pearls up to the sunlight.

I wrote a dialogue of about twenty-four pages entitled 'Cleanthes or the Starting-Point and Necessary Progress of Philosophy'. Here art and science, which had become completely separate regained to some extent their unity, and I vigorously set about the job itself, a philosophical and dialectical development of the divinity as it manifests itself as idea-in-itself, religion, nature and history. My last sentence was the beginning of Hegel's system, and this work for whose sake I had made some acquaintance with natural science, Schelling and history, which had caused me endless headaches and is written in so confused a manner (for it had actually to be a new logic) that I can now scarcely think myself back into it, this my dearest child, reared by moonlight, like a false siren delivers me into the arms of the enemy.

My vexation prevented me from thinking at all for several days and I ran like a madman around the garden beside the dirty waters of the Spree 'which washes souls and makes weak tea'. I even went on a hunting party with my landlord and rushed off to Berlin and wanted to embrace every street-loafer I saw....

My vexation at Jenny's illness, my fruitless and failed intellectual endeavours and my consuming anger at having to make my idol a view that

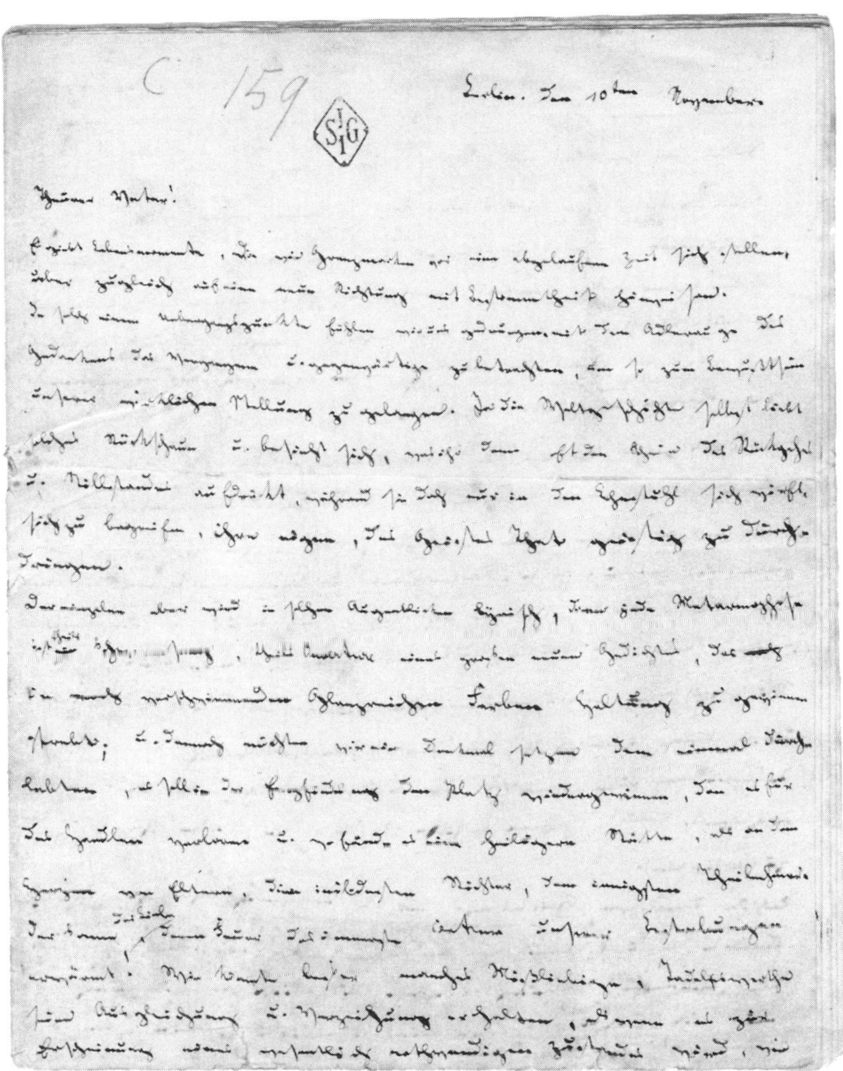

The beginning of Marx's famous letter to his father

I hated, made me ill, as I have already written to you, dear father. When I recovered I burnt all my poems and sketches for novels, etc., fancying that I could be completely free from them, which has at least not yet been disproved.

During my illness I had got to know Hegel from beginning to end, together with most of his disciples. Through several gatherings with friends in Stralow I obtained entrance into a graduate club among whose members were several university lecturers and the most intimate of my Berlin friends,

> Dr Rutenberg. In the discussions here many contradictory views appeared and I attached myself ever more closely to the current philosophy that I had thought to escape, but all the rich harmonies were stilled and a veritable fit of irony came over me, as was quite natural after so much negation. To this was added Jenny's silence and I could not rest until I had acquired modernity and a contemporary scientific outlook through a few bad pieces like *The Visit*.
>
> If perhaps I have not here described clearly to you the whole of this last term, nor gone into all the details and slurred the nuances, let my excuse, dear father, be my desire to talk of the present.

The gentle, worldly father must have been worried by the impetuous, passionate way in which his son dealt with different branches of knowledge and the problems of the modern world; he was bound to recognize that his son's demon was 'of a Faustian nature'. The alarm he felt was expressed in complaints, which for the sake of clarity he formulated as questions; he then went on to answer these questions 'entirely *a posteriori*' on the basis of real experience. He analyses his son's situation in great detail. According to him the problem is: what must his son do, if he respects his parents and if, without considering his age and his situation, he binds his fate with one of the noblest of young women and forces a 'very respectable family' to approve of a relationship which is full of dangers and dismal prospects for the beloved child? 'I shall give a prosaic answer based on real life as it actually is, at the risk of appearing a trifle too prosaic in the eyes of my respected son.' He is angered by his own weakness of character and feels himself growing into a peevish old man, 'who complains about his everlasting disappointments, and complains particularly because he has got to hold up in front of his idol a mirror full of distortion'. All the son's obligations constituted 'such a firmly woven bond that it would be necessary to exorcize all evil spirits, to banish all aberrations, make up for all shortcomings, and develop new and better motives; make a wild young man into an orderly person, convert a negating genius into a genuine thinker, and make a dissolute ringleader of depraved ruffians into a sociable man....' How did the son solve the problem?

> God help us!!! Everything in disorder, a sort of gloomy drifting around in all the branches of knowledge, dark brooding by a dull oil-lamp; degeneration in a scholarly nightshirt and with uncombed hair instead of degeneration with a glass of beer; a frightening lack of sociability and a disregard for all good manners, even of any respect for one's father.... And is it here in this scene of senseless and ineffective study that the fruits are supposed to ripen that will delight yourself and your dear ones? Is it here that the

Berlin University

harvest will be gathered that will help you to fulfil your sacred duties?! … I refuse to weaken for I feel I have been too indulgent, and thus to some extent I am as guilty as you. I must tell you that you have been a great trouble to your parents and brought them little joy. Scarcely had your wild behaviour in Bonn come to an end, scarcely was the ledger of your faults wiped clean – and truly there were all kinds of faults – when to our consternation there came the troubles of love; and then like good old parents in a story-book we became heralds and crusaders for that love. Yet since we feel deeply that your life's happiness is at stake, we endured the inevitable and perhaps even played unsuitable roles.… Occasionally we received a rhapsodic sentence or two that told us what our too fondly beloved son was really thinking and doing. Several times we were left for months without a letter, and on the last occasion you knew very well that Eduard was sick, that your mother and I were in pain, and in addition there was cholera raging in Berlin. And as if this was not even worth an apology, your next letter said not a word about it; instead it contained a few badly written lines and an extract from your journal, entitled *The Visit* – one which I would very much sooner turn away from my door, a crazy concoction that simply recounts how you waste your talents and stay up at nights to produce your incoherent rubbish. You are following in the footsteps of the new monsters that mumble their words until they can no longer hear themselves speak; they have only confused ideas or none at all, and so a flood of words is described as the birth of a genius.

Special attention is devoted to the high expenditure of the son. For some time the father had been ill – he suffered from the hereditary family illnesses, liver complaints and tuberculosis – and six months later he died. He doubted whether his fortune would be enough to provide for the large family. In Bonn the father had paid his son's debts without grumbling. But during the first years in Berlin the boy became altogether too careless with money. 'Just as if we were made of money, in one year Your Highness has gone through almost 700 taler, contrary to any agreement or any custom, whereas the very richest do not spend 500. But why? I do you the justice of thinking that you are no spend-thrift. But of course how can a man, who every fortnight or so invents new systems and then has to destroy all the work that has given him so much trouble – how can such a man be bothered with trifles? ...' In any case, in the same year the young Freiligrath, who was eight years older, wrote that he thought he could 'manage quite well on 180 to 200 talers' – and a Berlin town councillor received 800 talers a year. The son felt himself to be misjudged, and his father wrote again on 10 February:

> I am not going to keep on defending myself, and especially not when it comes to abstract reasoning, for I should first have to study the terminology before I could approach this sacred subject, and I am too old for that. If your conscience is in agreement with your philosophy, then I am glad to hear it. But there is just one point on which transcendent things are no help at all and it is precisely on this point that you have very shrewdly chosen to maintain a complete silence. I mean the paltry subject of money; you do not seem to know how much this means to the father of a family, but I have a better idea, and I tell you frankly that I occasionally reproach myself for having been much too weak in giving you your own way. We are now in the fourth month of the law year, and already you have had 280 talers. I have not yet earned as much as that this winter. Yet you unjustly say or imply that I am misjudging you. This is not true at all. I give you full credit for your feelings and your morality. I gave indisputable proof of this during the first year of your law studies when I refrained from insisting on an explanation about a very mysterious matter although it seemed highly dubious. Only a real belief in your moral feelings could have achieved this and, thank God, I am still of the same opinion. But I am not blind, and it is only from weariness that I lay down my weapons. Still you must always believe firmly that you have a place in the inmost recesses of my heart and that you are one of the strongest supports of my life....

The conflict with his father was not just a dispute between a young genius and a bourgeois father. Of course, the latter was alarmed by the way his son's development was tending towards violent extremes. But it is clear that his criticisms would have had a different tone if his son had

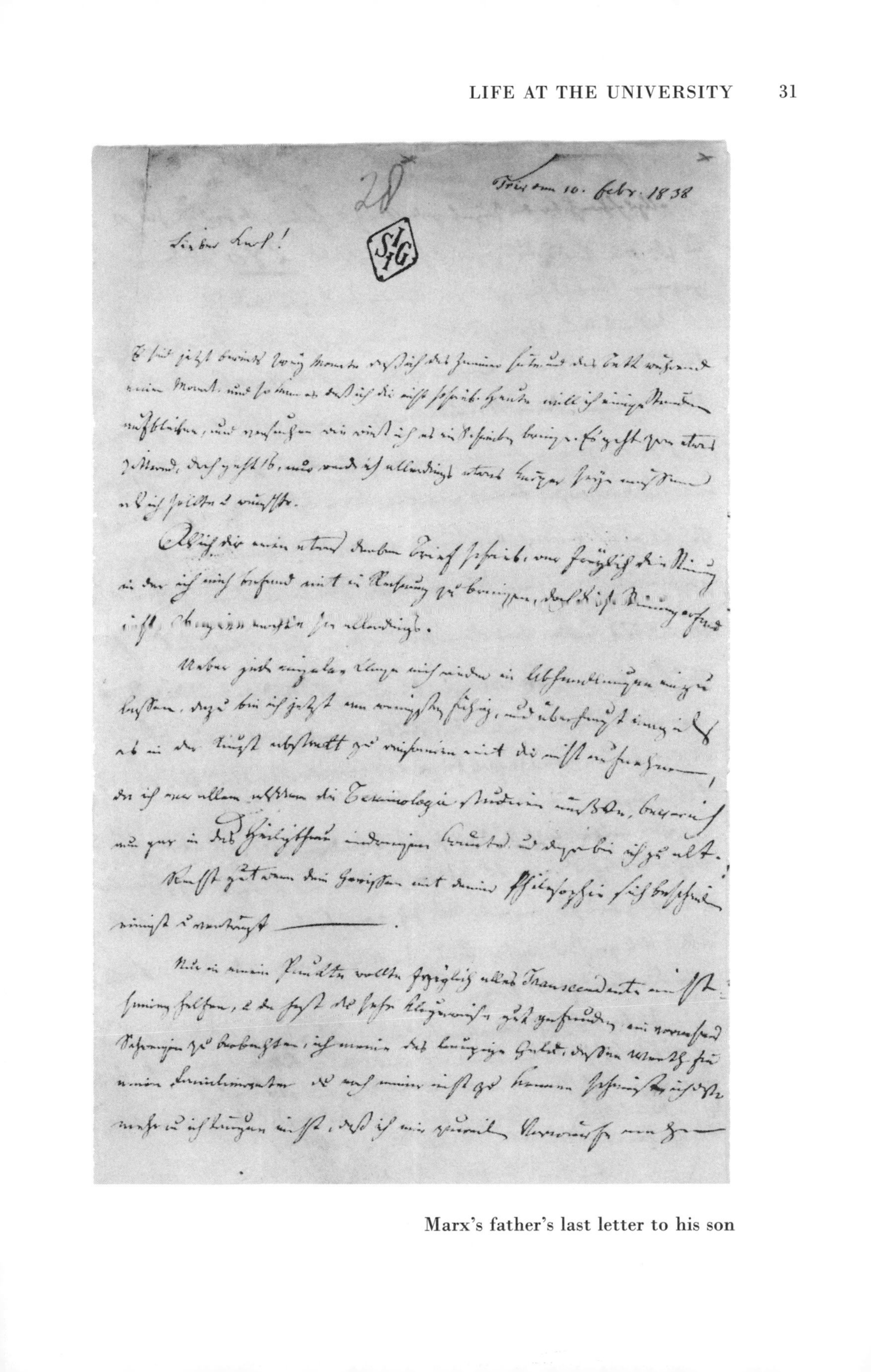

Trier am 10. Febr. 1838

Lieber Karl!

Marx's father's last letter to his son

not contracted a romantic attachment in Trier. For the son this was primarily a romantic experience, whereas for the father it represented a serious bourgeois engagement with clear-cut consequences. But the son was not yet in a position to become involved in this way.

This conflict was the central personal experience for Marx as a young man. In his later correspondence with Engels he frequently complains about his intimate relationships with others. But never again did he expose himself to another in a manner that was so ruthlessly open, so naively trusting, so lacking in pose or pretence, so free from all cynicism and so unrestrained, as he did in that ecstatic letter of confession to his father. The latter's remonstrances must have affected him deeply. He withdrew more and more and eventually developed a dread of personal avowals. Later, Marx was often to listen to reproaches similar to those of his father, but on that first occasion they were made by a clear-sighted and loving father, which is so strikingly obvious from the letters. His father's death on 10 May 1838 put an end to a conflict in which one of them was bound to be crushed – undoubtedly the father.

For Marx this severed his ties with his family. Even his relationship with his mother altered. In October 1838 she sent him 160 talers which he had requested. In May 1840 she complains, in the last letter to her son that has survived, of unfriendly treatment by the Westphalens. She says to him: 'You will never make the moral sacrifice for your family that we all made for you', and in a postscript she adds, 'I want to know whether you have taken your degree.' From that time on, if his mother is ever mentioned it is only in connection with money matters. Yet the picture of a hard-hearted miserly mother who abandoned her son when he was in need, is a legend that has even been fostered by Marx himself. The truth is that she repeatedly came to his assistance with quite substantial sums.

4

IN THE RANKS OF THE YOUNG HEGELIANS AND THE LIBERALS

During the early Berlin period, Marx busied himself with experiments in poetry and with legal studies. We may assume that the interest in philosophy which was soon to dominate him was awakened in the company of the members of the 'post-graduate club', who – above all Bruno Bauer and Friedrich Köppen – were to exert a strong influence on his intellectual development for several years. Marx did not acquire his philosophical education in the lecture-room. The 'post-graduate club' was soon associated with Arnold Ruge and the *Hallische Jahrbücher*, and it took a leading part in the Young Hegelian movement. The club represented the philosophical and political avant-garde.

Soon after Hegel's death his school began to disintegrate as the new trends of the period began to show themselves. After the July Revolution of 1830 liberal demands for a constitution and for the freedom of the press became more urgent. In one or two states, Saxony, Hanover and Kurhessen, they met with some success. The Hambach festival of 1832 initiated a new demagogic persecution. This was followed in 1835 by the suppression of the 'Junge Deutschland' movement which gave vivid expression to the feelings of the time, reflected above all in the writings of Heine, Börne and Gutzkow. Economic recovery, assisted by the expansion of communications and the founding of the Zollverein, increased the desire for political unification to follow on the creation of economic unity. As bourgeois self-awareness became stronger, liberalism was bound to become more radical. But the Prussian state reinforced political and religious reaction to serve as a protective dam against the revolutionary flood of liberalism, so that liberalism was forced to fight the state in its actual form.

Hegel believed that the state was 'the complete realization of the Spirit in existence', 'the Divine Idea in so far as it is existent on earth'.

G.W.F. Hegel

For him the State was 'What is rational in and for itself'; it was 'the absolutely supreme phenomenal form of the Spirit'. Since Hegel talked of the 'so-called people', it was difficult for a liberal to see how the State was also going to succeed in translating freedom into reality. The battle of liberalism against the Prussian state was bound to direct itself against Hegel's philosophy of the State, and this was responsible for the dominant role of this 'world philosophy' in the official philosophy of the Prussian state. Rudolf Haym described it correctly as 'the scientific incorporation of the spirit of the Prussian restoration'. Nor did people fail to note that Hegel had denounced the liberal-minded Professor Fries of Jena because of his opinion that in a State where the universal mind was dominant, 'life came from below, from the people', and also that Hegel considered any further reflection about the State as 'the restless activity of vanity'. Hegel's attitude was bound to be regarded as 'a scientifically formulated justification of the Karlsbad police-system and the demagogic persecution'.

The liberal critics directed their attack against the reactionary side of Hegel's philosophy, namely its justification of the existing state of affairs.

Marx's student friend Köppen (caricature by Engels)

According to Hegel's view philosophy had come to an end in his system; the future was of no interest to him. But it was towards the future that the thoughts of the young people were directed. And it was possible for them to continue the fight against reaction along the lines of Hegel's thought, in the sense in which they understood it; for his philosophy had a revolutionary side to it. This was the dialectical method, which stood opposed to the well-rounded completeness of his system; for the dialectical method did not view the world and events as being finished and completed, but as being uninterrupted processes in which everything, actuality as well as thought, is subject to the continual alteration of becoming and decay. Since it was easier for the censorship to suppress political radicalism, the battles took place in the theological and philosophical sphere.

Whilst his friends in the postgraduate club were about ten years older than Marx and were more knowledgeable than him, he excelled them in the boldness of his thought, in his wealth of ideas and in a certain vehement activism. When he had left Berlin in the spring of 1841, his friend Köppen wrote to him in Bonn to declare how much he had always been stimulated by contact with him: 'Once again I now have thoughts of my own, ideas that I have (so to speak) produced myself, whereas all my earlier ones came from some distance away, namely from the Schützenstrasse [where Marx lived]. Now I can really work once more, and I am pleased to be walking around amongst complete idiots without feeling that I am one myself.... As far as the ideas from the Schützenstrasse are concerned, our Bruno Bauer has written a splendid article in the *Hallische Jahrbücher*, not the least bit jesuitical. There this venerable gentleman starts by introducing the idea that the Byzantine State is the real Christian one; I subjected this idea to police-examination, and asked to see its passport, whereupon I observed that it too emanates from the Schützenstrasse. So you see, you are an absolute storehouse of ideas, a complete factory or (to use Berlin slang) you have the brain of a swot....' Next year when Friedrich Engels joined the circle of Berlin friends and wrote doggerel verses describing Bruno Bauer's battle against theology and the Church, he introduced Marx as one of Bauer's henchmen; not yet knowing Marx personally, he used Edgar Bauer's description of him:

Who comes last, wild and free?
A black lad from Trier now we see.
Grimly he strides, rising on his heel,
Foaming with rage, as if he would steal
The tent of the sky and drag it to earth,
Stretching his arms high in his mirth.
His fist is clenched, he rages without compare,
As if ten thousand devils had him by the hair.

During the next few years Marx was exclusively preoccupied with the philosophical studies of his subject; the intensity of these may be gathered from the Dissertation, and particularly from his copious preliminary work. At the beginning of 1839, he took as his special subject research into Late Greek Philosophy, for which there were practically no auxiliary resources at all. The subject of the Dissertation was 'The Difference between Democritus's and Epicurus's Philosophy of Nature', and as late as 1842 he was thinking of extending it into a long general account of the Epicurean, Stoic and Sceptic philosophies. 'The time has now arrived, when the systems of the Epicureans, the Stoics and the Sceptics can be properly understood. They are the philosophers of self-consciousness' it said in the Preface to an edition which he planned. Marx and his friends had also arrived at 'a philosophy of self-consciousness'; and in the present intellectual situation, characterised by the termination of philosophy in Hegel's system, there was a strong parallel with the way in which mat-

Bruno Bauer

erialistic philosophy appeared after Greek Philosophy had been brought to completion by Aristotle. In the Preliminary Notes to the Dissertation we find the following account of this, his own situation, which already contains the seeds of the later dispute with the Young Hegelians. Hegelian philosophy, which presents itself as a complete and total world in which idea and reality are blended together in absolute harmony, is faced with actual reality whose petty restrictedness makes it seem a hostile contrast.

> The world is thus split, but it is faced with a philosophy that is a totality in itself. The way in which this philosophy is seen to act is therefore also split and contradictory; its objective universality gets turned round into subjective forms of the individual consciousness in which it is alive and active.... Anyone who does not understand this historical necessity, must as a result deny that it is possible for men to live at all in accordance with a total philosophy; or else he must hold the dialectic of proportion to be the highest category for a mind cognizant of itself, and must, together with some of those who misunderstand Hegel, maintain that *mediocrity* is the normal appearance of the absolute mind....

Marx considers it incorrect to explain a number of weaknesses in the Hegelian system (as many Hegelians do) as a 'compromise' with reality, i.e. usually political reality; it seems to him necessary to analyse Hegel's ideology itself:

> It is conceivable that a philosopher should be guilty of this or that inconsistency; he may himself be conscious of it. But what he is not conscious of is that in the last analysis this apparent compromise is made possible by the deficiency of his principles or an inadequate grasp of them. So if a philosopher really has compromised, it is the job of his *followers to use the inner core of his thought to illuminate his own superficial expressions of it*. In this way, what is a progress in conscience is also a progress in knowledge. This does not involve putting the conscience of a philosopher under suspicion, but rather construing the essential characteristics of his views, giving them a definite form and meaning, and thus at the same time going beyond them.... It is a psychological law that once the theoretical intellect has achieved freedom within itself it turns into practical energy and, emerging from the shadow kingdom of Amenthes as *will*, directs itself against the exterior reality of the world.... Its relation to the world is one of reflection. Being inspired with the desire to realize itself, there is a tension between it and other things. Its inner self-sufficiency and perfection are destroyed. What was an inner light becomes a consuming flame that turns outwards. As a consequence, the world's becoming philosophical coincides with philosophy's becoming worldly, the realization of philosophy coincides with its disappearance, and the exterior battles of philosophy are against its own inner deficiencies....

Marx expresses his fanatical love of truth, his determined ruthlessness towards external conditions, in the following form:

> Philosophy, as long as it still has one drop of blood in its all-conquering and absolutely free heart, will always cry out to its enemies, like Epicurus: 'Godlessness consists, not in destroying the gods of the mob, but in attaching the opinions of the mob to the gods.'

Prometheus' avowal in Aeschylus's tragedy, 'I harbour hatred against all the gods', is philosophy's declaration 'against all gods in earth and heaven that do not recognize human self-consciousness as being the supreme godhead'. For him Prometheus is 'the greatest saint and martyr in the philosophical calendar'.

Since the Preliminary Notes were becoming increasingly voluminous, Bruno Bauer, who since 1839 had been a *privatdozent* in Bonn, urged Marx to complete the work, so that he too could qualify as a university lecturer in Bonn: 'If you could only acquit yourself properly in this, then you will have triumphed. I wish I could only get to Trier in order to explain things to your people. I believe the small-town atmosphere

Arnold Ruge

tends to make for complications.... Your fiancée is capable of enduring anything with you, and who knows what is to come? I think the day of reckoning is coming nearer and nearer, insofar as it will mean an open breach....' Bauer's premonitions were to be confirmed; his criticism of the Gospels, which went far beyond Strauss and viewed the Gospels as being the literary products of the Evangelists and Christianity as being a product of the Graeco-Roman world, brought his dismissal. Nor could Marx continue to think of an academic career. But for his fiancée and her family it became urgently necessary that he should at last finish with his studies. He handed in his Dissertation to the philosophical faculty of Jena on 6 April 1841 and he was awarded his doctorate on 15 April.

Just as in Berlin Marx was recognized by older friends as being the chief among them and the most gifted, so too he was in Bonn. Moses Hess, who was six years older, described him enthusiastically to his friend Berthold Auerbach: 'You can prepare yourself to meet the greatest philosopher now living, perhaps the only one.... Dr Marx (for that is the name of my idol) is still quite a young man, about 24 years of age at the most, and he is about to deal the finishing stroke to medieval religion and politics. He combines the most profound philosophical seriousness with a cutting wit. Imagine for yourself Rousseau, Voltaire, Holbach, Lessing, Heine and Hegel, united in one person – and I say *united*, not just thrown together – then you've got Dr Marx.'

Instead of a professorial chair, he found a platform in the *Rheinische Zeitung*, a newspaper that had appeared in Cologne since 1 January 1842; it was founded by a group of wealthy liberal citizens, Georg Jung, Dagobert Oppenheim, Gustav Mevissen, and others. The contributors mostly came from the Berlin circle of the Athenians, which took the place of the post-graduate club and later styled itself 'The Free Men': Bauer, Köppen, Meyen, Stirner, Rutenberg and Engels. Marx's articles at once aroused great interest, and on 15 October he took over the editorial direction of the newspaper. Looking back on this time later, Marx said:

> It was during the years 1842-43, as editor of the *Rheinische Zeitung*, that I first found myself in the predicament of having to join in the discussion about so-called material interests. It was the negotiations of the Rhine Landtag regarding the theft of wood and the parcelling up of real estate, the official polemic concerning conditions among the Moselle peasants which Herr van Schaper (then President of the Rhine Province) launched against the *Rheinische Zeitung*, and finally the debates about free trade and protective tariffs that first caused me to occupy myself with economic questions.

Such was the importance of these articles; even more significant for Marx himself was the discussion about Communism which the newspaper was forced to conduct.

Earlier contacts with social questions had not left their mark on Marx's mind. When Councillor von Westphalen, who was enlightened in social matters, sought to get him acquainted with Saint-Simon, he would certainly have heard something about Ludwig Gall, the German social reformer who, from Trier in the twenties, began to spread the ideas of Owen, Fourier and Saint-Simon. Emphasis had also been laid on the Saint-Simonists by Eduard Gans, the Berlin lecturer who had had the greatest influence on Marx. In Gans's book that appeared in 1836, *Glances at Persons and Events of the Past*, he asserted:

> But amidst all this intellectual confusion the Saint-Simonists have said something of importance, and have put their finger on a public scandal of the day. They have correctly observed that slavery has not really disappeared; though it has been formally prohibited, in practice it still exists in the fullest form. Once there was the opposition between master and

> slave, then between patrician and plebeian, and later still between feudal lord and vassal; now we have the idle rich and the worker. One only has to visit the factories of England and one will find hundreds of men and women, emaciated and wretched, sacrificing their health and all the pleasure of life, even their meagre subsistence, in the service of one man. Is this not slavery when man is exploited like an animal, even if he might be free to die of hunger? ... It is a profound insight into our times that the State must care for the poorest and most numerous class; that if it wishes to work it should never lack suitable employment; that one of our principal aims must be to reduce that crust of society which is usually called the 'rabble'. It will be more necessary now for future history to speak of the struggle of the proletariat against the middle classes. The Middle Ages with their guilds had a proper organization for labour. The guilds have been dissolved and can never be set up again. But are the forces of labour, once liberated from the corporation, to fall into the hands of despotism? To escape the dominion of masters only to succumb to that of factory-owners? Is there no remedy for this? Yes, to be sure. It lies in association and the free corporation.

At the beginning of the forties in Germany – to say nothing of France – there was a huge quantity of literature about the social question. There is no sign that Marx took any interest in this before his time in Cologne. He considered himself a philosopher, even though he was now concerned with political and philosophical matters that were quite different from the Late Greek Philosophy he had studied. He was indeed now championing the 'impoverished, and politically and socially dispossessed masses'; but it is certain that indignation over social injustice did not take first place with him, as it did for instance with Engels in the case of the social grievances of the pietistic Wuppertal. Nor was he like the young Lassalle, who was so filled with indignation by the Jewish persecution of 1840 in Damascus, that he wanted to liberate the Jews, and later the entire nation. The high standard of the young Marx's journalistic work was much more the result of a compelling logic and a subtlety in antithesis, based on a philosophical training.

It was not so much concern for the liberal character of the *Rheinische Zeitung* that caused him to reject the 'allusions to communism' which his Berlin contributors introduced. Marx was frightened that:

> By their political romanticism, vainglory and boastfulness, they might compromise the success of the party of freedom.... I called for them to show less vague reasoning, fine-sounding phrases, conceited self-admiration and more precision, more detail on concrete circumstances and more knowledge of the subject. I explained that I held the smuggling into incidental theatre-reviews, etc., of communist and socialist dogmas, that is of a new world-view, to be unsuitable and indeed immoral, and that I

> desired quite a different and more profound discussion of communism if it were to be discussed at all,

he wrote to Ruge. To Dagobert Oppenheim he expressed himself in favour of moderation:

> Such a forthright demonstration against the basic pillars of the State could provoke increased censorship, or even the suppression of the newspaper. That was how the *Süddeutsche Tribüne* fell. But in any case we shall upset many (and perhaps most) free-thinking practical men, who have adopted the painful course of battling for freedom step by step, within constitutional limitations, if we sit comfortably and demonstrate their inconsistency.

When the *Augsburger Allgemeine Zeitung* accused the Cologne newspaper of communist sympathies, he replied with the following declaration of principle:

> The *Rheinische Zeitung* does not even concede *theoretical validity* to communist ideas in their present form, let alone desires their practical realization, which it anyway finds impossible, and will subject these ideas to a fundamental criticism. If it had aims and capacities beyond well-polished phrases, the *Augsburger* would have perceived that books like those of Leroux and Considérant and, above all, the acute work of Proudhon cannot be criticized by superficial and transitory fancies but only after consistent and probing study.... We are firmly convinced that the true danger does not lie in the practical attempt to carry out communist ideas, but in their *theoretical development*; for practical attempts, *even by the masses*, can be answered with a *cannon* as soon as they have become dangerous, but ideas that have overcome our intellect and conquered our conviction, ideas to which reason has riveted our conscience, are chains from which one cannot break loose without breaking one's heart. They are demons that one can only overcome by submitting to them. Yet the *Augsburger Zeitung* has never got to know the *crisis of conscience* caused by the rebellion of man's subjective desires against the objective insights of his own reason....

Judging by their high moral tone as well as their classic style, these sentences might well come from Lessing, for whom ideas were also forces of destiny which demand an act of conscience. Marx's intellectual honesty required that one should make a more thorough study of communism before saying anything about it. He could not declare himself in favour of it unless it corresponded exactly with his views. This showed the need for a critical examination of Hegel's Philosophy of the State, which Marx now proceeded to tackle. His approach to communism followed a rational and logical development; it was to be the decision of a passionate thinker. For who else could speak of a *crisis of conscience* produced by ideas?

Marx as Prometheus (a contemporary allegory of the banning of the *Rheinische Zeitung* in 1843)

The *Rheinische Zeitung* was the newspaper that was most persecuted by the censorship. A ministry presided over by the King decided that the newspaper was to be suppressed on 1 April; on 18 March Marx announced that he was resigning as editor 'on account of the present attitude of the censorship'. He wrote to Ruge:

> It is hard to fight for freedom and to be forced to use needles instead of clubs. I am getting tired of all the hypocrisy, stupidity and crude authority, and yet at the same time of all our softness and hair-splitting and refusal to see the truth.... In Germany there is nothing more I can do. One is simply betraying oneself here.

A decisive battle for liberalism was impossible in Germany. Marx clutched eagerly at an offer from Ruge to take part in a review that was being started abroad, in succession to the *Deutsche Jahrbücher* that had also been prohibited. Ruge wrote: 'I think we can largely maintain the substance of the *Jahrbücher* and rely on a much stronger market, provided we give a thorough treatment to politics and publicism, and at the same time get rid of the doctrinaire element.' Under these circumstances it might well provide Marx with as much as 850 talers a year. This referred to the *Deutsch-Französische Jahrbücher* which were to appear in Paris. Marx was very pleased about the offer:

> As I have already told you several times, I have quarrelled with my family and, as long as my mother is still alive, I have no right to my inheritance. Besides I am engaged to be married, and I cannot and will not leave Germany without my fiancée.

Even though Marx had not pressed on with his studies on account of his fiancée, there had been no change in her feelings towards him. All her life long, even at the cost of great sacrifices, she adapted her life to his. Even in Trier, 'the most wretched little hotbed of gossip and ridiculous scandal', she had much to put up with. Marx wrote to Ruge:

> Finally, I will also inform you of what my private plans are. As soon as we have completed the contract, I want to go to Kreuznach and get married and stay there a month or more with my bride's mother, because in any case before we get to work we shall have to have some pieces of work ready.... I can assure you without any romanticism that I am head over heels in love in all earnestness. I have already been engaged for over seven years and my bride has fought the hardest of fights for me that have almost undermined her health.... I and my bride have thus fought through years of more unnecessary and exhausting conflicts than many others who are three times as old as we are and continually speak of their 'experience of life' (the favourite phrase of our *juste milieu*).

On 12 June the marriage contract was signed in Kreuznach. Marx stayed in Kreuznach until the end of October. He prepared himself for Paris by studying French history and philosophy, and in addition he was engaged on a critique of Hegel's *Philosophy of Right*, as well as his essays for the *Jahrbücher*.

5

THE POWER OF NEW IDEAS: COMMUNISM

When Marx arrived in Paris in November 1843, he already found himself close to communism, which he only found himself justified in believing when it presented itself as a logical philosophical development. He agreed with what Friedrich Engels wrote the same month in *The New Moral World*: 'Communism, however, was such a necessary consequence of New Hegelian philosophy, that no opposition could keep it down.' When the critique of Hegel's philosophy of the State led Marx, via Feuerbach, to communism, these 'new ideas' took possession of him with a demonic energy. When he had reached the new standpoint, he immediately planned, with a real mania for systems, to make it the basis of a new system. At any rate he signed a contract with the publisher Leske in Darmstadt, for a two-volume work entitled *A Critique of Politics and Economics*. It never came out because Marx, together with Engels, had to explain the new standpoint in a number of polemical works in order to clarify his own position and distinguish it from other socialist tendencies. In the sixties the publisher reminded him that the advance had got to be repaid.

It was of the greatest importance for Marx to be able to study French socialists and revolutionary history. He also met well-known socialists, to whom Moses Hess introduced him; yet the only one with whom he seems to have been more intimate for a time was Proudhon, against whom he later directed one of his fiercest polemics. The Frenchmen invited to collaborate in the *Jahrbücher*, which its founders had tried to make into a kind of 'intellectual Holy Alliance', bringing Germany and France closer together, rejected the offer on account of the project's atheism. Marx lived chiefly in his study. Germans he kept as far as possible at a distance; there were about 85,000 of his countrymen in Paris at the time, mostly intellectuals and migrant artisans who had been drawn to the 'Capital of

Freedom'. On the other hand Marx occasionally visited meetings of French workmen, and these made a great impression on him.

> When the communist artisans meet, they seem to be meeting for the purpose of propaganda, etc. But in the process they also acquire a new need, the need for society, and what seemed to be a means has become an end in itself. One can see the most illuminating effects of this practical process if one watches a meeting of socialist French *ouvriers*. Smoking, drinking and eating are no longer merely an excuse for meeting. The society, the entertainment, which is supposed to be for the purpose of meeting, is sufficient in itself; the brotherhood of Man is no idle phrase but the real truth, and the nobility of Man shines out at us from these faces brutalized by toil.

For a time Marx and his wife lived with the Ruges in the Rue Vanneau, in a 'communist community' set up by them for reasons of convenience. This experiment soon failed. Ruge did not like the spirit of Marx's essays for the *Jahrbücher*; he always remained a liberal, and besides was very narrow-minded. The quarrel was accentuated by personal antipathy. It is from those months that we are indebted to Ruge (in a letter to Feuerbach) for a glimpse of Marx's life that may not be altogether untrue: 'He reads a great deal; he works with extraordinary intensity and has a talent for criticism, which occasionally degenerates into dialectic. But he never finishes anything; he is always breaking off, and then plunges again into an infinite ocean of books.... He may well have been born to be a scholar and a writer, but as a journalist he is a complete failure.' Ruge may have meant by this that Marx wrote very clumsily and felt he needed to make copious notes for his articles.

Marx's relations with Heinrich Heine were friendly, and for some time Heine was under his influence. The line in the poem to Hans Christian Andersen, 'Ich hab' ein neues Schiff bestiegen mit neuen Genossen' ('I have boarded a new ship with new comrades') refers to the communist doctrine and the circle around Marx – Ruge, Hess, Bakunin and Herwegh. During the next few years Heine wrote a number of poems with a communist point of view, as well as some of his bitterest political satires, like 'The Silesian Weavers' and 'Deutschland, ein Wintermärchen'. The idea that the rebellion of the weavers was a general uprising, and that the revolt was not merely due to hunger, was the argument used by Marx against Ruge and is also that of the poem.

When Marx was ordered out of Paris he wrote to Heine: 'I should very much like to take you along with me.' What attracted Heine to the communists was not their attitude towards private ownership – he rejected this, just as he had done that of the Saint-Simonists ten years before – but their atheism. Later, he returned to a quasi-deist position. Heine can hardly be described as a communist, and must have seen his new friends as being, above all, allies in the fight against Prussia. In 1854, in his *Retrospektive Aufklärung*, Heine mentioned that Marx had consoled him in 1848 after an attack by the *Augsburger Allgemeine Zeitung* which had flared up over Heine accepting a pension offered him by the French government. In opposition to Engels Marx defended Heine's right to it, declaring they had once been friends: Heine was doing this 'with a bad conscience; for the old dog has a marvellous memory for that sort of rubbish'.

Even in his Dissertation, Marx recognized that the 'termination', i.e. the 'realisation', of philosophy was a contemporary problem. This was the starting point of his critique of Hegel. It was probably in 1841 that he started his critique of the section 'State Right' in Hegel's *Philosophy of Right*, and he continued the work in 1843 when he offered Ruge an essay on the subject for the *Deutsche Jahrbücher*. This huge manuscript, prepared as preliminary notes, was left unfinished. Marx follows the method of Feuerbach's critique of speculative philosophy, which the latter had formulated in his *Vorläufige Thesen zur Reformation der Philosophie*: 'All we need to do is always make the predicate into the subject, and make the subject into the object and principle – that is to say, reverse the speculative philosophy; and then we have the undisguised, pure and clear truth.' Marx follows this principle quite logically. His only objection to Feuerbach's *Theses* was that the book 'said too much about nature and too little about politics. But this is the only combination by which present-day philosophy can attain truth.'

He directed his main attack against Paragraph 262 of the *Philosophy of Right*, about which he says, 'The entire mystery of the *Philosophy of Right* and of Hegelian philosophy in general is contained in these paragraphs.' In Hegel, the State, 'the actual idea, the Spirit', is divided into two spheres, the family and civil society. As against this view of the family and civil society as being 'the dark natural ground from which the light of the State emerges', Marx sets 'the actual relationship', pleading the authority of ordinary human understanding. For obviously the State only exists on the basis of the family and society: 'The political State cannot exist without the natural basis of the family and the artificial basis of civil society; they are its *conditio sine qua non*.' In Hegel

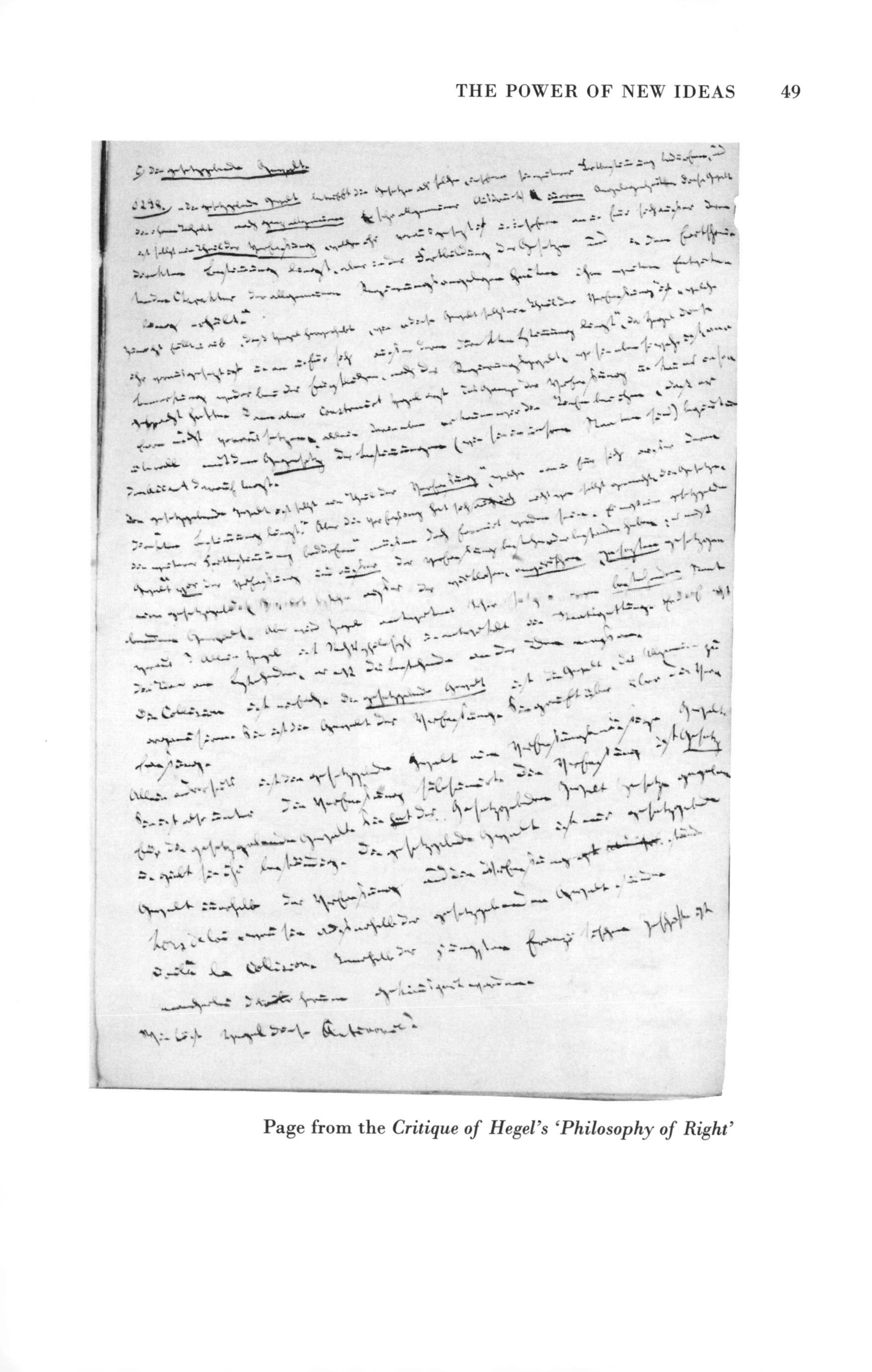

Page from the *Critique of Hegel's 'Philosophy of Right'*

this condition is itself made conditional on the idea of the State; the idea becomes the subject, and the real subject (the family and civil society) is made the predicate: 'It is important that Hegel always makes the idea into the subject, and the real subject ... into the predicate.'

The correctness of this proposition is shown paragraph by paragraph, and thus the 'mystification' of Hegel is unveiled. For him,

> what is essential to determine political realities is not that they can be considered as such but rather that they can be considered, in their most abstract configuration, as logical-metaphysical determinations. Hegel's true interest is not the philosophy of right but logic.... The philosophical moment is not the logic of fact but the fact of logic. Logic is not used to prove the nature of the State, but the State is used to prove the logic.

For Hegel, 'the sovereignty of the people is one of the confused notions based on the wild idea of the "people"'. As against this Marx says firmly:

> The 'confused notions' and the 'wild idea' are only here on Hegel's pages. ... For the State is an abstraction; the people alone is the concrete. The people is the real State.... In monarchy the whole, the people, is subsumed under one of its modes of existence, the political constitution; in democracy the constitution itself appears only as one determination, and indeed as the self-determination of the people. In monarchy we have the people of the constitution, in democracy the constitution of the people. Here the constitution ... is returned to its real ground, actual man, the actual people, and established as its own work.... Man does not exist because of the law but rather the law exists for the good of man.... That is the fundamental difference of democracy.

In a real Community there is no contradiction between the *political State*, which in the constitution and as bureaucracy is distinguished from the real life of the people as something external and alien, and the life of the people. One can say with the new French writers that 'in true democracy the political State disappears'. True democracy is not yet the republic; for there the people sees even the constitution as being something 'transcendental' and alien. Only when private and public existence have become identical will it be possible to speak of true democracy, identical with the 'classless society', as Marx was later to call it.

On the basis of this critique Marx was able to proceed to the decisive breakthrough in the critique of politics which he accomplished in the *Jahrbücher* essay, 'Introduction to a Critique of Hegel's *Philosophy of Right*'. Hitherto, the Germans had only thought what other nations had done. Marx asks himself whether Germany can attain a praxis, i.e. a

DEUTSCH-FRANZÖSISCHE

JAHRBÜCHER

herausgegeben

von

Arnold Ruge und Karl Marx.

1ste und 2te Lieferung

PARIS,

IM BUREAU DER JAHRBÜCHER. } RUE VANNEAU, 22.
AU BUREAU DES ANNALES.

1844

Title-page of the *Deutsch-Französische Jahrbücher*

revolution, that will raise her not only to the level of modern nations, but to the human level which will be the immediate future of these nations. He knows very well that:

> It is clear that the arm of criticism cannot replace the criticism of arms. Material force can only be overthrown by material force; but theory itself becomes a material force when it has seized the masses. Theory is capable of seizing the masses when it demonstrates *ad hominem*, and it demonstrates *ad hominem* as soon as it becomes radical. To be radical is to grasp things by the root. But for the man the root is man himself.... The criticism of religion ends with the doctrine that *man is the supreme being for man*. It ends therefore with the *categorical imperative to overthrow all those conditions* in which man is an abased, enslaved, abandoned, contemptible being....

Marx sees the positive possibility of this German emancipation in the creation of a class with radical chains:

> A class must be formed which has *radical chains*, a class in civil society which is not a class of civil society, a class which is the dissolution of all classes, a sphere of society which has a universal character because its sufferings are universal, and which does not claim a *particular redress* because the wrong which is done to it is not *a particular wrong* but *wrong in general*.... Which is, in short, a *total loss* of humanity and which can only redeem itself by a *total redemption of humanity*. This dissolution of society, as a particular class, is the *proletariat*. The proletariat is only beginning to form itself in Germany, as a result of the industrial movement. For what constitutes the proletariat is not naturally existing poverty, but poverty *artificially produced*.... Just as philosophy finds its *material* weapons in the proletariat, so the proletariat finds its *intellectual* weapons in philosophy. And once the lightning of thought has penetrated deeply into this virgin soil of the people, the Germans will emancipate themselves and become men.... In Germany *no* type of enslavement can be abolished unless *all* enslavement is destroyed. Germany, which likes to get to the bottom of things, can only make a revolution which upsets *the whole order* of things. The *emancipation of Germany* will be an *emancipation of man*. *Philosophy* is the *head* of this emancipation and the *proletariat* is its *heart*. Philosophy can only be realized by the abolition of the proletariat, and the proletariat can only be abolished by the realization of philosophy.

While Marx was proclaiming with such high moral feeling the alliance between philosophy and the proletariat, he was trying out his critical methods on an unsuitable subject in the two *Jahrbücher* essays, 'On the Jewish Question'. These are polemical articles attacking Bruno Bauer who saw only one possible way of securing Jewish emancipation, for which the Jews were fighting a hard battle: their emancipation from their religion. Marx naturally saw this as a social problem, and not a religious and political one. Here too he felt the real subject was the split between the political State and civil society – the difference between restricted political liberation and a general human liberation. He did not want to deal with the sabbath-Jews, but with the everyday-Jews. 'Let us not seek the mystery of the Jew in his religion; let us rather seek the mystery of the religion in the actual Jews.' He sees the worldly basis of Judaism in self-interest; he sees commerce and money as its worldly god: 'The emancipation from commerce and money, that is to say from practical real Judaism, would be the self-emancipation of our time.' This theme was developed further with some degree of sophistry. Quite rightly all Jewish scholars have resisted this attempt to identify Jewishness with stockbroking. And the real significance of these essays may be that they pose a psychological problem that is very important for Marx: namely, was he antisemitic?*

---

* See for example E. Silberner, 'Was Marx an Antisemite?' in *Judaica*, XI, No. 1, April 1949.

The view that he was rests on these articles, on certain passages in other writings and on articles in the *Neue Rheinische Zeitung*, as well as on many statements about the Jews that are particularly frequent in the correspondence with Engels and which, far from being 'clever' and 'witty', are objectionable and tasteless. At the same time it is not correct to describe Marx as an antisemite. Nor does our generation need to be told that a view like that of Karl Vorländer, in his biography of Marx in 1929, must be firmly rejected; at that time, when Nazism was becoming popular, it was deemed advisable to lay particular emphasis on these statements of Marx, in order to defend him against being attacked as a Jew. As far as the essays are concerned, we must agree with Gustav Mayer that here Marx was rather unscrupulously trying to demonstrate the superiority of his new attitude over the ideological views of the Young Hegelians. But neither should it be forgotten that he treats the concrete social and political situation without any knowledge of the social and intellectual history of the Jews, and that he employs his method in an uncritical and purely logical fashion.

It is a different matter with the remarks in the correspondence; they belong to those parts of the correspondence which often make painful reading. The contemptuous tone in which Marx speaks of the Jews was not taken over from Engels, though certainly the latter found it quite easy to join in, and even Jenny Marx took to using the style in her letters. Nor was Marx's behaviour due (as Simon Dubnow thinks) to 'the renegade's characteristic dislike of the camp he has abandoned'; on the contrary, it was chiefly a typical expression of 'self-hatred'. In the past this feeling was the reaction to a hostile environment shown by sensitive natures who had freed themselves mentally from Judaism; and it was itself a product of antisemitism. We may think of Otto Weininger, who described this as a characteristic phenomenon, or of Theodor Lessing, who wrote about it in detail, to say nothing of lesser minds. It is remarkable that a personality such as Marx was unable to conquer this weakness all his life long. During his many feuds he was always particularly ferocious against those opponents who described him as a Jew – Ruge, Proudhon, Bakunin and Dühring. In December 1881 his son-in-law Longuet mentioned in an obituary for Jenny Marx that, before her marriage, considerable opposition, especially racial prejudice, had to be overcome in Trier, since Marx had been born a Jew. On the same day Marx declared angrily to his daughter Jenny Longuet that there had been *no* racial prejudice to overcome; he would be very grateful if 'Herr Longuet' would kindly not mention his (Marx's) name in his writings.

The proclamation of the alliance between philosophy and the proletariat created an urgent necessity for a detailed study of economics. Marx did not study economics because he was attracted by the material; he turned to it as a philosopher whose ideas centred on revolution and human emancipation, for which a valid theoretical basis was needed. The first and most important result of these efforts were what are widely known today as the *Economic and Philosophical Manuscripts*, written early in 1844, which were not intended for publication. They were not actually published until 1932, when they appeared simultaneously in Riazanov's *Collected Edition* of Marx and Engels, and in an edition of *Early Writings* edited by Siegfried Landshut. They at once created a great sensation, especially amongst philosophers and sociologists who could not understand the generally accepted view that, though Marx had certainly been a philosopher in his youth, he had soon 'overcome' this stage and by way of history had arrived at his proper sphere, that of economics. The early writings made it possible to place Marx's later work in its true, broad context. Herbert Marcuse's forecast that their publication would 'become a decisive event in the history of Marxist scholarship' has been fulfilled; now we try to understand Marx, not from *Capital*, but from these early writings in which Marx attempts to grasp the *total* situation of Man. His standpoint is that of a philosopher who at the same time *also* has to make himself into a historian, an economist and a political theorist.

In these early writings Marx wishes to provide a critique of economics and starts out from Hegel's *Phenomenology of Mind*, in which the categories – labour, objectification, alienation, and transcendence – acquire a new meaning.

> The greatness of Hegel's *Phenomenology* and its final product, the dialectic of negativity as the moving and creating principle, is on the one hand that Hegel conceives of the self-creation of man as a process, objectification as loss of the object, as externalization and the transcendence of this externalization. This means, therefore, that he grasps the nature of *labour* and understands objective man – true, because real, man – as the result of *his own labour*.

Whereas 'labour' here means activity of the mind and hence only purely intellectual labour, Marx thinks of it anthropologically as the labour of an actual man, a man who is acting in a particular situation, and not an abstract man dissociated from real life.

A page from the *Economic and Philosophical Manuscripts*

Once Marx has noted and digested the views of classical economists on such subjects as wages, the profit on capital, and rent, he applies the critique to *alienated labour*. In labour man objectifies his being, he externalizes himself in an object which then stands outside him as something alien to himself.

> The alienation of the worker in his object is expressed as follows in the laws of political economy; the more the worker produces the less he has to consume; the more value he creates the more worthless he becomes; the more refined his product the more crude and misshapen the worker; the more civilized the product the more barbarous the worker; the more powerful the work the more feeble the worker; the more the work manifests intelligence the more the worker declines in intelligence and becomes a slave of nature.... What constitutes the alienation of labour? First, that the work is *external* to the worker, that it is not part of his nature; and that, consequently, he does not fulfil himself in his work but denies himself, has a feeling of misery rather than well-being, does not develop freely his mental and physical energies but is physically exhausted and mentally debased. The worker, therefore, feels himself at home only during his leisure time, whereas at work he feels homeless. His work is not voluntary but imposed, *forced labour*.

The fact that the alienation of a man's labour deprives him of the object of his production, also has the effect of depriving him of his species-life; the latter expresses itself in his working over of the objective world, which nature makes into *his* work and his reality:

> An immediate consequence of this ... is the alienation of man from man. When man is opposed to himself, it is another man that is opposed to him. What is valid for the relationship of man to his work, the product of his work and himself, is also valid for the relationship of man to other men and their labour and the objects of their labour. In general, the statement that man is alienated from his species-being, means that one man is alienated from another as each of them is alienated from the human essence.

If the product of a man's labour is alien, then to whom does it belong?

> If the product of labour does not belong to the worker but stands over against him as an alien power this is only possible in that it belongs to *another man apart from the worker*.... Thus through alienated, externalized labour the worker creates the relationship to this labour of a man who is alien to it and remains exterior to it. The relationship of the worker to his labour creates the relationship to it of the capitalist, or whatever else one wishes to call the master of the labour. *Private property* is thus the product, result and necessary consequence of *externalized labour*, of the exterior relationship of the worker to nature and to himself. Thus private property is the result of the analysis of the concept of externalized labour, i.e. externalized man, alienated work, alienated life, alienated man.

In industry based on marketing and the distribution of labour, in which we are confronted with 'the objectified life-forces of man', this alienation has reached its peak and in money it receives its ultimate expression:

> It changes fidelity into infidelity, love into hate, hate into love, virtue into vice, vice into virtue, slave into master, master into slave, stupidity into intelligence and intelligence into stupidity....

But things are different when man is really *human*:

> If you suppose man to be man and his relationship to the world to be a human one, then you can only exchange love for love, trust for trust, etc.... Each of your relationships to man – and to nature – must be a definite expression of your real individual life that corresponds to the object of your will....

In the proletariat we see the 'complete loss of man'. Only if the proletariat transcends itself can man realize himself. Only after the transcendence of alienation will it be possible for man to have an existence that matches the essence and dignity of the human race.

Friedrich Engels in 1845

But a form of communism that aims at political emancipation and even wishes to transcend the State, yet allows private property 'or the alienation of man' to continue – such as that advocated by Proudhon and the so-called 'true' socialists – 'has not yet grasped the positive essence of private property or the human nature of needs'. Communism must be conceived of more widely and deeply:

> [To be] communism as the positive abolition of private property and thus of human self-alienation and therefore the real reappropriation of the human essence by and for man. This is communism as the complete and conscious return of man conserving all the riches of previous development for man himself as a social, i.e. human being. Communism as completed naturalism is humanism and as completed humanism is naturalism. It is the genuine solution of the antagonism between man and nature and between man and man. It is the true solution of the struggle between existence and essence, between objectification and self-affirmation, between freedom and necessity, between individual and species. It is the solution to the riddle of history and knows itself to be this solution.

In Hegel, the forms of alienation refer only to consciousness; therefore Hegel's system remains inside the sphere of alienation. In contrast to Hegel, Marx praises Feuerbach, 'the only person to have a serious and critical relationship to the Hegelian dialectic', for having recognized philosophy as being a 'form and mode of existence of human alienation'. He praised him for having 'founded true materialism' by making 'the social relationship of man to man the basic principle of his theory', and for having opposed Hegel's mere 'negation of the negation' with 'the positive that has its own self for foundation and basis'. Continuing to build on this foundation of 'real humanism', Marx created the theory of revolution, which aims to overthrow capitalist society in order to realize the human essence.

The most important event during the Paris period for Marx was the visit of Friedrich Engels – the beginning of their life-long friendship. Engels had contributed to the *Jahrbücher* an essay entitled 'An Outline of the Critique of Economy', which showed Marx how much further this young man (who was two years his junior) had advanced in this subject by studying English economic theory and practice. Engels, who was the son of a merchant in Barmen and was himself a merchant, had the experience in practical economics that Marx lacked. Later Marx repeatedly asked his advice on these questions. In their collaboration they were a perfect complement to each other. Whereas Marx could only express himself creatively after detailed study and systematic examination of the material and after a long struggle, Engels had an astonishing gift for speedy orientation. He was quick to disentangle a problem, and could express his views on it elegantly, effortlessly and yet forcibly. They were both in complete agreement about their ideas and at once set about developing them further, first of all in the dispute with the Bauer brothers in *The Holy Family*. In addition to the considerable critical gifts of the two authors and their self-confident sarcasm and facetiousness, *The Holy Family* (as are chapters in *The German Ideology* devoted to Bauer and Stirner) is characterised by what Mehring called 'bilious, quarrelsome and long-winded polemic', which often tries the patience of the reader. Memories of the abrupt way in which the *Rheinische Zeitung* rejected the 'Free Men' of Berlin (a group that included the Bauer brothers) determined the tone of the 'critical critique' and Marx's replies. For, in Bauer's own words, his *Allgemeine Literaturzeitung* was supposed 'to show up the liberalism and radicalism of the year 1842 in all their emptiness and incompleteness'. It was intended to replace the 'arrogant, malicious, petty, envious criticism' of the *Rheinische Zeitung* with a free and human type of criticism. Besides, claimed the Bauers, the *Rheinische Zeitung*'s move towards communism was only evidence of philosophical confusion. Engels assessed *The Holy Family* (in which Marx made considerable use of his economic and philosophical manuscripts) in the following letter to Marx:

> But altogether the thing is too big. The profound contempt that we both show towards the *Literaturzeitung* is an unhappy contrast with the 22 pages we devote to it. And in addition most of the criticism of speculation and abstraction in general will be unintelligible to the public at large and not even very interesting.

In January 1845, at the request of the Prussian government, Marx was expelled from France on account of two anti-Prussian articles in the Paris newspaper *Vorwärts*, which was also suppressed. Since a prosecution for high treason arising out of the *Jahrbücher* awaited him in Prussia, the Marx family went to Brussels with their daughter Jenny who had been born in 1844; there they were allowed to remain until February 1848. Marx had to give an undertaking that he would publish nothing on current politics. Since the Prussian police continued to show an interest in him, he surrendered his Prussian citizenship in December. Later on in England naturalization was refused him on the grounds that he had 'behaved disloyally towards his King'; henceforward he took no new nationality. In Belgium his family was increased by the birth of his daughter Laura and his son Edgar, the darling of the family, who later became a victim of their misery in London and lived only to the age of eight.

These years already produced a number of the financial difficulties which were to beset Marx all his life despite the generous assistance of Engels. During the last few years his Cologne friends Jung and Claessen had sent him a few thousand francs, and after he had been expelled from Paris, Jung organized a subscription for him in Cologne and Elberfeld which brought in a considerable sum. Engels too wanted to make a collection: 'At least the swine must not have the pleasure of getting you into financial trouble through their filthy tricks.' Most of the burden of this refugee life was borne by Frau Marx: 'My time is always meanly divided between big and small worries and all the cares and troubles of daily life.' But even this 'vagabond existence' had not destroyed her optimism.

The following incident will show how sensitive Marx was at this time about money. He was insulted when Joseph Weydemeyer, the most

Jenny Marx in 1834

intelligent and reliable of their agents in Germany, raised money for him among the Westphalian socialists, and he threatened to break off relations with that group. Weydemeyer pleaded that he must not look upon the money as charity; it was from party members who could not accept that their principal champion should be in need through no fault of his own. When Marx sent back the money because he was in the process of preparing an attack on those very socialists, Weydemeyer himself became irritated and, though he only laughed at 'Engels's dictatorial demands and lordly tone', he told Marx that he could not understand how the latter could make this a party matter, and that these were completely personal conflicts which had nothing to do with questions of principle. 'I would have thought our Party was split up enough without any more unnecessary divisions.' Later, Marx received a large advance on his paternal inheritance from his mother; this amounted to six thousand francs and was paid out to him at the beginning of 1848 through the mediation of his brother-in-law Schmalhausen.

Even as early as 1844 all kinds of socialist literature was to be found in Germany; newspapers and periodicals had prepared the ground for propaganda. It was for this reason that, in October of this year, Engels sent a warning to Paris: 'Until the principles have been logically and historically developed from the previous way of looking at things and from previous history, and until the necessary continuation of the same has been set out in a few articles, everything will continue to be a kind of daydream and, for most people, a blind fumbling-about.' And in January 1845: 'Hurry up and get your book on economics finished. Even if there are parts you are still not satisfied with, that doesn't matter. People are ready for it and we must strike while the iron is hot.' With exaggerated optimism he reported enormous successes; at meetings in Elberfeld he had noticed that it was something altogether different to speak to real live men, from what it was 'to go on with this cursed abstract writing to an abstract public that one simply imagined with one's mind's eye'. Weydemeyer too was pressing Marx to finish the *Economics*, as one had no idea what to give to people who were dubious about the possibility of communism; and in the *Jahrbücher* and *The Holy Family* the development was only hinted at.

But first of all Marx needed further to clarify and illustrate his view of history. This he did in collaboration with Engels in *The German Ideology*, a refutation of Feuerbach, Bauer, Stirner and so-called 'true socialism', a chiefly philosophical and emotional form of communism predominant in Germany. Even this considerable work was not issued in full until the publication of the *Early Writings* in the nineteen thirties. At the time it was written there was no possibility of it being printed – although Engels issued the warning: 'Every month that we hold these manuscripts up, they will lose 5 to 10 francs in exchangeable valuta' – and the authors were obliged to abandon them to 'the gnawing criticism of the mice'. *The German Ideology* is important because it gives a detailed treatment of what Engels was later to call 'the materialist view of history'. Ten years later Marx clearly stated its fundamental idea in the well-known, indeed banal formulation in the Preface to *A Contribution to the Critique of Political Economy*:

> In the social production which men carry on they enter into definite relations that are indispensable and independent of their will; these relations of production correspond to a definite stage of development of

Die heilige Familie,

oder

Kritik

der

kritischen Kritik.

Gegen Bruno Bauer & Consorten.

Von

Friedrich Engels und Karl Marx.

Frankfurt a. M.

Literarische Anstalt.

(J. Rütten.)

1845.

Title-page of *The Holy Family*

their material powers of production. The totality of these relations of production constitutes the economic structure of society – the real foundation, on which legal and political superstructures arise and to which definite forms of social consciousness correspond. The mode of production of material life determines the general character of the social, political, and spiritual processes of life. It is not the consciousness of men that determines their being, but, on the contrary, their social being determines their consciousness. At a certain stage of their development, the material forces of production in society come in conflict with the existing relations of production, or – what is but a legal expression for the same thing – with the property relations within which they had been at work before. From forms of development of the forces of production these relations turn into their fetters. Then occurs a period of social revolution. With the change of the economic foundation the entire immense superstructure is more or less rapidly transformed.... The bourgeois relations of production are the last antagonistic form of the social process of production.... At the same time

Ludwig Feuerbach

> the productive forces developing in the womb of bourgeois society create the material conditions for the solution of that antagonism. With this social formation, therefore, the prehistory of human society comes to an end. Only then will the history of 'genuinely human' society begin.

Everything in Marx's development now pressed on towards revolutionary practice. He had already emphasized it in his *Theses on Feuerbach*:

> Man must prove the truth, i.e. the reality and power, the 'this-sidedness' of his thinking in practice.... The philosophers have *interpreted* the world in different ways; the point is to change it.

In order to put into practice this alteration of the world, it was necessary to find some method of associating for political activity. Here Engels was the driving force. In Paris he had for some time cleverly engaged in discussions and intrigues in the groups of the League of the Just; but his efforts to reduce the influence of the 'true' socialists had met with very little success.

With Marx, the unconditional quality and ruthless logic that characterize his thought took the form of intransigence in political activity. In this

5–7 rue d'Alliance, where Marx first lived in Brussels

respect he was never very successful. It is difficult to imagine Marx and Engels as leaders of a party; for this they lacked the most important requirement: the art of handling men. There was something curt and off-putting in their manner. Engels wrote: 'Here in Paris I have become accustomed to a very impudent tone, for strumming suits the business, and it goes a long way with the petticoats.' But this kind of corps-student's cynicism is not kept only for the 'petticoats'; he refers to the workmen of the trade unions as 'roughnecks' and 'louts'. Marx, too, had taken over much of this tone; they always used this way of describing the proletariat. Even if this is not taken too seriously, it was never a quality that made it easy to achieve contact with people. Moreover, as with the proletariat and louts and roughnecks, the two friends did not always distinguish clearly between sociological categories and their own personal classification; 'bourgeois' and 'Philistine' are generally used as synonyms, and the latter did not refer only to the narrow-minded.

The Russian Paul Annenkov, who visited Marx during this period in Brussels, leaves a graphic description of him:

> He was typical of the kind of man who is made up of energy, will-power and unshakable conviction, a type that is highly remarkable even at first glance. With a thick black mane of hair on his head, his hands covered with hairs, his coat buttoned up awry, he nevertheless gave the appearance of a man who has the right and the power to command attention, however odd his appearance and his actions might seem. His movements were awkward, but bold and self-confident; his manners ran positively counter to all the usual social conventions. But they were proud, with a trace of contempt, and his harsh voice which rang like metal was curiously in keeping with the radical judgements on men and things that he let fall. He always spoke in imperative phrases that would brook no resistance; moreover his words were sharpened by what seemed to me an almost painful tone which rang through everything that he said. This tone expressed a firm conviction that it was his mission to dominate other minds and prescribe laws for them. I was faced with the incarnation of a democratic dictator, such as one's imagination might have created.

Annenkov wrote this description after a meeting at which Marx mercilessly disposed of the 'apostle of communism', Wilhelm Weitling. This journeyman-tailor, an eloquent and devout believer in a just world-order, was no match against Marx's acid philosophical dialectic. But his defeat was only incidental to Marx's elimination of all the trends of German socialism that existed prior to the Revolution of March 1848. This was done in the *Deutsche Brüsseler Zeitung* and in the circulars issued by the Communist Correspondence Bureau, through which Marx and his friends maintained communication with the English Chartists and the various groups of the League of the Just. Lithographed circulars were issued in which, according to Marx:

> ...the scientific study of the economic structure of bourgeois society was shown to be the only tenable theoretical basis; it was finally explained in a popular form that it was not a question of implementing some kind of utopian system, but of consciously participating in a visible historical revolution of society.

It goes without saying that in these disputes Marx triumphed over all his opponents. Even a few years later the gentle Moses Hess recalled his experiences: 'It is a pity, a terrible pity that this man, who is easily the most gifted member of our Party, is too proud to be content with all the recognition he has earned from those who know and value his achievements; it is a pity he seems to demand a kind of personal submission which I for one will never concede to any man.'

Moses Hess

Usually this kind of theoretical altercation meant that Marx 'disposed of' his opponent even as a person, so that there could never again be any personal relationship with him. This happened with Proudhon in 1847 after the publication of *The Poverty of Philosophy*. Amongst other things Marx reproached him with changing economic categories into 'pre-existing eternal ideas', instead of 'taking them to be theoretical expressions of a historical stage, a particular developmental stage, of the productive-relationships corresponding to material production.' Later on Marx maintained:

> Proudhon naturally inclined towards dialectic. But since he never understood the really scientific type of dialectic, he only succeeded in producing sophistry. In practice this was in keeping with his petty-bourgeois point of view. The petty-bourgeois is ... made up of 'on the one hand' and 'on the other hand'. This is so in his economic interests, and therefore also in his politics, in his religious, scientific and aesthetic opinions. So it is in his morality, in everything. He is a living contradiction....

Wilhelm Weitling

Proudhon noted in his diary that Marx often distorted his meaning or deliberately misunderstood him. Moreover he accused him of plagiarism.

This accusation was made by Marx against many others, as well as by others against Marx. Amongst others Linguet, Saint-Simon, Sismondi, Thierry and Mignet have all been cited as intellectual ancestors of Marx's theory of history, and his socialist opinions have been fathered on a number of French socialists. Anarchists have even described the *Communist Manifesto* as a plagiarism of Considérant, and have cited a number of identical or similar phrases as 'proof' The same happened later with Marx's economic theories. But no intellectual achievement is ever made in complete isolation, and similarity of expression only goes to prove that the time is ripe for a particular idea. It was Marx's achievement to work over and assimilate many earlier elements into a creative synthesis. Nor was he afraid to recognize what he owed to others; for example, on 5 March 1852 he wrote to Weydemeyer:

MISÈRE

DE

LA PHILOSOPHIE.

RÉPONSE A

LA PHILOSOPHIE DE LA MISÈRE

DE M. PROUDHON,

Par Karl Marx.

PARIS.
A. FRANK,
69, rue Richelieu

BRUXELLES.
C. G. VOGLER,
2, petite rue de la Madeleine.

1847

Title-page of *The Poverty of Philosophy*

Pierre-Joseph Proudhon

> I do not deserve the credit for having discovered either the existence of the classes in modern society, or the struggle between them. Long before me bourgeois historians had shown the historical development of this class struggle, and bourgeois economists had shown the economic anatomy of the classes. What I did that was new, was to prove: 1. that the existence of classes was merely tied up with certain definite historical developmental struggles of production; 2. that the class-struggle necessarily led to the dictatorship of the proletariat; and 3. that this dictatorship itself was only a transition towards the abolition of all classes and towards a classless society.

The London Central Committee of the League of the Just, which in summer 1847 changed its name to the Communist League, had become converted to Marx's views; and, at a congress in London in November, Marx and Engels were commissioned to prepare a manifesto for the League. Engels made a draft in the form of a confession of faith. A catechism was the literary form usually used at that time, when workers were given socialist enlightenment in the shape of question and answer.

Engels's draft was later published by Eduard Bernstein as *Principles of Communism*. At the end of November Engels approached Marx: 'Think over the confession of faith. I believe we had better drop the catechism form and call the thing: *Communist Manifesto*. As more or less history has got to be related in it the form it has been in hitherto is quite unsuitable....' The *Manifesto* contains nothing that the authors had not already said in other works; but in it they made their ideas intelligible to anyone and assembled them in precise and monumental language, free from any Hegelian phraseology. The suggestive power of the style played a large part in placing this work in the front rank of historical manifestoes; in the nineteenth century there was none to equal it. It is an explosive appeal – not a compendium of sociological conclusions. The authors soon noted that it was no longer quite up to date; in August 1852 Engels wrote to Marx: 'California and Australia are two cases that were not provided for in the *Manifesto*: huge markets created out of nothing. They must go in.'

Over the following decades they discovered much that was lacking; but quite rightly they made no additions, for in its original form the work had exerted a historical influence. Its direct effect could not of course be very great; for the *Manifesto* appeared in an edition of only a thousand copies, and the organization of the movement was only in its very earliest stages. On the other hand, the date of publication, February 1848, gave a special actuality to its anticipation of revolution and its formulation of the tasks of Communists during the German Revolution:

> In Germany they fight *with* the bourgeoisie whenever it acts in a revolutionary way, against the absolute monarchy, the feudal squirearchy, and the petty bourgeoisie. But they never cease, for a single instant, to instil into the working class the clearest possible recognition of the hostile antagonism between bourgeoisie and proletariat, in order that the German workers may straightaway use, as so many weapons against the bourgeoisie, the social and political conditions that the bourgeoisie must necessarily introduce along with its supremacy, and in order that, after the fall of the reactionary classes in Germany, the fight against the bourgeoisie itself may immediately begin. The Communists turn their attention chiefly to Germany, because that country is on the eve of a bourgeois revolution that is bound to be carried out under more advanced conditions of European civilization, and with a much more developed civilization, and with a much more developed proletariat, than that of England was in the seventeenth, and of France in the eighteenth century, and because the bourgeois revolution of Germany will be but the prelude to an immediately following proletarian revolution.

Manifest

der

Kommunistischen Partei.

Veröffentlicht im Februar 1848.

Proletarier aller Länder vereinigt Euch!

London.

Gedruckt in der Office der „Bildungs-Gesellschaft für Arbeiter"
von J. E. Burghard.
46, Liverpool Street, Bishopsgate.

Title-page of the *Communist Manifesto*

Above all as a result of his lapidary pronouncement that it was an inescapable fact that social development must follow a regular pattern, Marx has been more and more ranged with the Old Testament Prophets. This line had been taken before by scholars who questioned the scientific character of Marx's theories; this was the case with all the Jewish scholars, and in our own time with Camus and Borkenau or the theological interpreters. This meant disregarding the most essential characteristics of the old type of prophecy:* the view that there is no such thing as inescapable fate; that a nation creates its own destiny, and that God does no more than accomplish human will; that a prophet only wants to establish a regular connection between the present and the future and to proclaim a reward or punishment for good or bad behaviour; and that therefore prophecies only have a conditional character, and that a prophet's certainty about the future is only a moral certainty.

None of this can be found in Marx. Of course there are character traits which are not unjustifiably often quoted as examples: the profoundest intellectual absorption in and experiencing of current events; an obsession with 'vocation', which leaves the prophet no choice but to speak or be silent, and which is the real secret of the prophetic personality; the claim to exclusivity and infallibility (Marx himself, writing to Engels on 25 August 1851, extolled the 'Communists' pride in infallibility' as a great virtue); and finally, fanaticism: 'All those whom Marx attacked – and whom did he not attack? – condemned the stubborn fanaticism with which this solitary man, heedless that practically no one wished to listen to him, clung to a single idea; they condemned the inconceivable frenzy which never allowed him to doubt that this single idea would triumph, even after it had been defeated. Where else do we find examples of such a rigid faith, which his contemporaries thought laughable but which posterity finds sublime, save among the prophets of Israel and Judah?'†

Marx himself would have indignantly rejected any such comparison in no uncertain terms. And yet the keystone of his view of history, the element in his theories that has exerted by far the strongest influence, is the coming revolution and the messianic role of the proletariat, whose victory will abolish for ever all class domination and will make possible

* See for example the fine interpretation by E. Auerbach in *Die Prophetie* (Jüdischer Verlag, Berlin, 1920).

† Gustav Mayer, 'Der Jude in Karl Marx', in *Neue Jüdische Monatshefte*, 25 April 1918.

for the first time a *truly human* society. Here Marx abandoned the territory of experience; yet for him this 'prophecy' had all the certainty of scientific knowledge. By combining the elements revealed by economics and socialism he intuitively grasped the developmental tendencies of bourgeois society. But the philosophical logician in him could not rest content with indicating its tendencies; he had to weld them together into a solid theory which could provide a strong basis for action against this society. He achieved this systematic development with the help of the dialectic in which, by transposing Hegel's formula to the course of history, he saw an infallible means of understanding the great epochs of human history and their relation to one another, and of acquiring knowledge of the laws of the previous course of history. He believed this method to be so infallible and so precise that he thought it would allow him to forecast the future and determine the final goal of history.

6

1848 – REVOLUTION AS IDEA AND REALITY

The idea that revolutions were 'the locomotives of history' fascinated Marx. For him, the contradictions immanent in society were so developed that a political revolution was bound to detonate an 'explosion', to lead to a proletarian revolution. In revolutions whole epochs were crammed together into weeks. Later, speaking of 'the bourgeois attitude of the English workman', he remarked to Engels:

> Only the little German petty-bourgeois, who measures world history by the yard and the latest 'interesting news in the paper', could imagine that in developments of such magnitude twenty years are more than a day – though later on days may come again in which twenty years are embodied.

The outbreak of the February Revolution in Paris, on 24 February 1848, must have greatly encouraged Marx. To him it was unimportant that he and his wife were arrested at night by the Belgian police and expelled. The new French government reversed Guizot's expulsion order, and invited Marx to Paris, where he arrived in time to oppose Herwegh's plan to liberate Germany from its rulers with the aid of a German legion, and was able to restrain the Communists from the undertaking which ended in the defeat at Niederdossenbach. In Paris Marx formed a new Central Committee of the Communist League, and he got it to draw up a programme for Germany – seventeen 'Demands of the Communist Party'. Revolution had not yet taken place in Germany: on 13 March it was successful in Vienna, and on 18 March in Berlin.

As far as Germany was concerned, the *Communist Manifesto* laid down the general rules: the Communists were to fight alongside the bourgeoisie against feudalism and the petty-bourgeoisie, stressing all the time the intrinsic opposition of the two temporary allies, so that the fight against the bourgeoisie could begin immediately after their victory. In Germany

Public funeral of the victims of the March Revolution in Berlin, 1848
(painting by Adolph von Menzel)

the bourgeois revolution must be immediately followed by the proletarian revolution. Though this was the tactic that sprang from the *Manifesto*, the actual demands were formulated in the Seventeen-Point Programme. These were different from those in the *Manifesto*, since they were intended as demands on a bourgeois-parliamentary regime. However they include: (1) Germany to be a single indivisible republic; (2) arms to the people; (3) active and passive electoral rights for all adult men; (4) abolition of all feudal burdens without indemnity; (5) all estates, mines, collieries, and public transport, as well as mortgages on peasant land, to become the property of the state; (6) a single state bank instead of private banks; (7) the salaries of state employees only to be differentiated according to their family situation; (8) restriction of the right of inheritance; (9) national workshops; and (10) free education for the people. In 1884 Engels remarked: 'Never has a tactical programme proved as successful as this one.' By this he must have meant that many of these demands later became the common property of all socialist programmes. In that particular revolution the programme was not of course realized. What then was the real situation in Germany with reference to these demands and those of the *Manifesto*?

As far as the élite of the Communist League was concerned, on 14 January of that year Engels gave Marx a description when he wrote from Paris, which contained the largest proportion of those who could really be called Communists: 'Things with the League here are in a wretched state. I have never seen such sleepy-headedness and petty jealousy as amongst these fellows. Weitling's and Proudhon's ideas are really the furthest these idiots will go, and so there is nothing to be done. Some are real roughnecks, louts of old men, and the others would-be petty-bourgeois.'

In the same month the sober Weydemeyer reported from Westphalia that in the second United Landtag the following year, the bourgeoisie would be bound to be victorious over feudalism, and that, until then, reaction would start in the most impertinent fashion.

> But the saddest thing is that, in this battle between absolutism and the bourgeoisie, our Party cannot distinguish itself, indeed a proper party leadership is quite impossible. We cluster in little groups on all sides, that is to say in any place where a leader knows how to collect around himself the few revolutionary elements of the young bourgeoisie.

And at the same time:

> As regards propaganda, I am placing most of our hopes on the railways, which will soon be crossing our district of Westphalia in all directions. They will at last bring some movement into this dead and isolated life. There are many powerful elements scattered in little corners, but until then they will all be swamped in philistinism because they have only been associating with philistines. Now it is easy for us to meet. Then things will be quite different.... Even England will grant us a little space to develop an industrial proletariat, and it will all be different. In Westphalia at least the first spinning-machine has already been set up.

For Marx, the 'Party' of the *Communist Manifesto* was not made up of the small meetings of the League; he saw it rather as a proletarian class-movement *in the broad historical sense*. But even this did not exist in Germany; it was scarcely possible to discern its crude outlines. At the end of April Engels was forced to write from Barmen to Marx at Cologne: 'At bottom the thing is that these radical bourgeois here too see in us their main future enemies and do not want to put any weapons into our

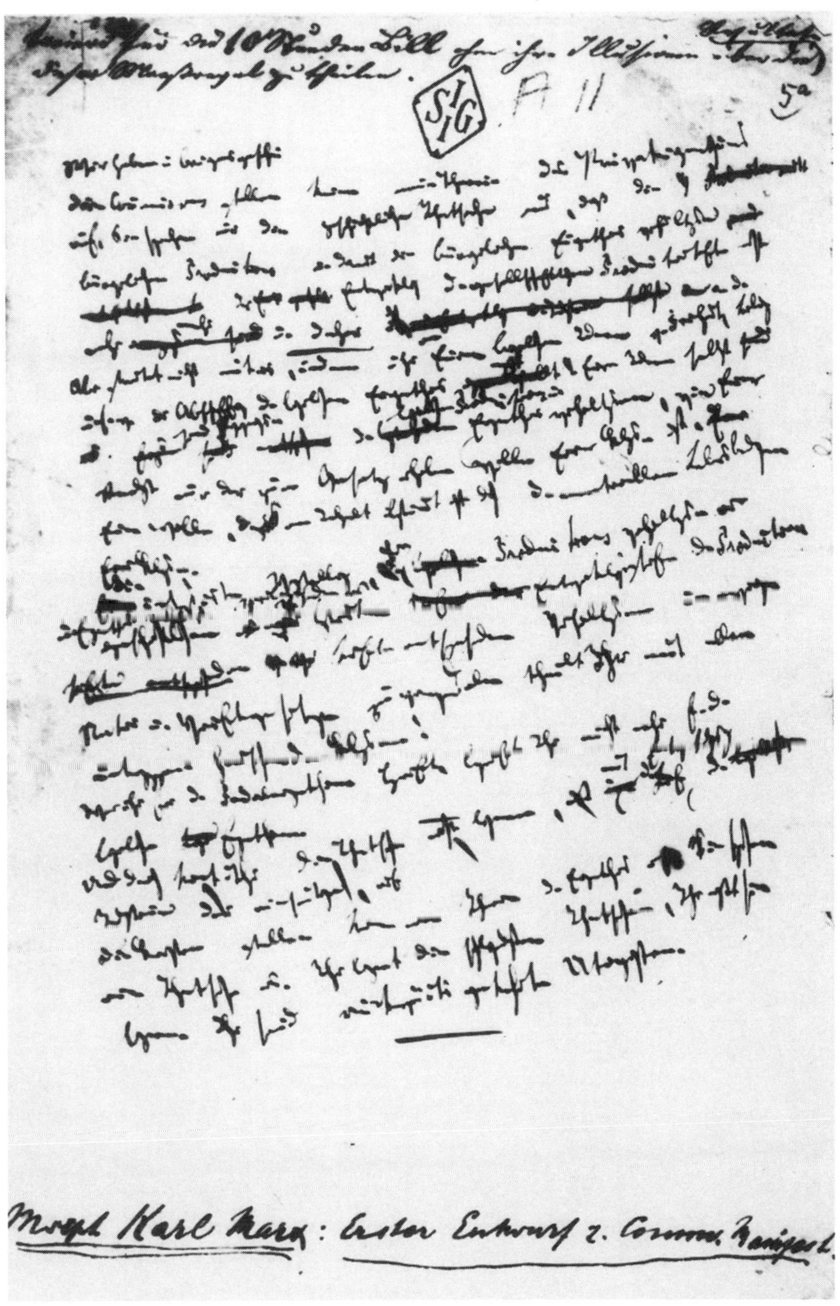

First draft of the *Communist Manifesto*

hands which we should very soon turn against them ... If a single copy of our Seventeen Points were to be distributed here, then all would be lost. The bourgeoisie here is totally abject.' And the workers?

> The workers are beginning to stir themselves a little – still very crudely, but massively. They have straightaway begun making coalitions. Of course this just gets in our way. The Elberfeld political club ... firmly rejects any debate on social questions, although in private these gentlemen admit that these questions ought now to be on the agenda, at the same time remarking however that we must be careful not to jump the gun!

Among Marx and Engels's closest friends in Brussels was Stephan Born, a compositor and contributor to the *Deutsche Brüsseler Zeitung*, who left immediately for Berlin as soon as the workers rose there on 18 March. He reports that he felt himself: 'suddenly freed of all the ideas he had had when at a distance.... In a moment all Communist ideas vanished for me, they seemed to have no connection at all with what the present required.' Born became the chairman of a kind of trade-union central committee, the forerunner of the Workers' Brotherhood, the great workers' organization of this period. The programme of this committee stated: 'that in a nation which, though it may contain workers as well as poor and oppressed people, has no working *class*, there can never be a revolution.... If we wish to make it a fact that we exist as a working class, as a power in the state, ... then the *organization* of the workers must be our principal task.'

Such evidence, much more graphic than the corroborative statistics, shows that in Germany there was neither the classic bourgeoisie nor the proletariat which, with all their contradictory development, are presumed to exist in the *Communist Manifesto*. It was therefore completely impossible that a bourgeois revolution in Germany should be followed immediately by a proletarian revolution.

At the beginning of April, Marx and Engels met in Cologne. With great difficulty the necessary shares were collected in order to launch the *Neue Rheinische Zeitung*. On 31 May the paper was able to appear as 'the Organ of Democracy', according to its subtitle. Marx was the chief editor; he determined the policy of the newspaper, in fact his guiding spirit was discernible in everything. In Engels's words, the constitution of the newspaper was 'simply dictatorship by Marx'. With the aid of a number of versatile contributors – Engels, Dronke, Weerth, and Wolff – he succeeded in making it into a first-class fighting newspaper. It came out until 18 May 1849, and with its 301 numbers it is not only the best

Neue Rheinische Zeitung.

Organ der Demokratie.

№ 1. Köln, Donnerstag, 1. Juni 1848.

Die „Neue Rheinische Zeitung" erscheint vom 1. Juni an täglich.

Der Abonnementspreis beträgt: Für das Vierteljahr in Köln 1 Thlr. 15 Sgr.; für alle übrigen Orte Preußens 2 Thlr. 3 Sgr. 9 Pf. Außerhalb Preußens mit Zuschlag des fremden Zeitungsporto's.

Das Abonnement für den Monat Juni kann nur unter gleichzeitiger Bestellung des nächsten Quartals (Juli, August, September) geschehen. Der Preis dieses viermonatlichen Abonnements beträgt: Für Köln 2 Thlr.; auswärts 2 Thlr. 25 Sgr.

Man abonnirt bei allen Postanstalten und Buchhandlungen des In- und Auslandes; — für Köln in der Expedition der Zeitung bei Hrn. W. Clouth, St. Agatha 12, Köln.

Fernere Aktienzeichnungen werden entgegen genommen in der Expedition der Zeitung. Auswärtige werden gebeten, sich ebenfalls dorthin franco zu wenden.

Insertionsgebühren.

Für die vierspaltige Petitzeile oder deren Raum . . . 1 Sgr. 6 Pf.

Die Expedition der „Neuen Rheinischen Zeitung."

Das Erscheinen der Neuen Rheinischen Zeitung war ursprünglich auf den ersten Juli festgesetzt. Die Arrangements mit den Correspondenten ꝛc. waren auf diesen Termin getroffen.

Da jedoch bei dem erneuten frechen Auftreten der Reaktion deutsche Septembergesetze in naher Aussicht stehen, so haben wir jeden freien Tag benutzen wollen, und erscheinen schon mit dem ersten Juni. Unsre Leser werden es uns also nachsehen müssen, wenn wir in den ersten Tagen an Nachrichten und mannigfaltigen Correspondenzen noch nicht das reichhaltige Material liefern, wozu unsere ausgedehnten Verbindungen uns befähigen. In wenig Tagen werden wir auch hierin allen Anforderungen genügen können.

Redaktions-Comité.

Karl Marx, Redakteur en Chef.

Heinrich Bürgers,
Ernst Dronke,
Friedrich Engels,
Georg Weerth,
Ferdinand Wolff,
Wilhelm Wolff,
} Redakteure.

Uebersicht.

Deutschland. Köln (die Frankfurter Versammlung. — Robert Blums Erklärung. — Preußische Staatsanleihe. — Hüser). — Berlin (Baldenaire.) — Frankfurt (die Nationalversammlung). — Wien (neue Revolution).

Belgien. Brüssel (die belgische Konstitution).

Italien. Verona (vom Kriegsschauplatz). — Neapel (Auflösung der Deputirtenkammer).

Frankreich. Paris (Absetzung von Thomas. — Fortschritte der Reaktion. — Commission für die Nationalwerkstätten. — Gerücht über eine neue Revolution in Neapel).

England. London (O'Connor, Cobden, Hume. — Mitchells Verurtheilung).

Handels- und Börsennachrichten.

Amtliche Nachrichten.

Bekanntmachung.

Deutschland.

Humoristische Skizzen aus dem deutschen Handelsleben.

Von Georg Weerth.

Der Herr Preiß in Nöthen.

Wiederum stehen wir im Comptoire des Herrn Preiß. Röthlich strahlt der Morgen durch zwei große, halbverstaubte Fenster auf die Dintenkleckse des Schreibpultes. Sandbüchsen, Federmesser, Gänsekiele und ähnliche friedfertige Instrumente schlummern in holder Gemeinschaft neben Postpapier und Propatria. ...

First number of the *Neue Rheinische Zeitung*

newspaper of that revolutionary year; it has remained the best German socialist newspaper. But its significance went beyond propaganda. In accordance with their tactical principles, the Communists linked up with the democratic clubs in order to speed up the bourgeois movement. Soon after his arrival Marx dissolved the Communist League. Since there was no possibility of reaching agreement about this, he did it simply on the basis of his dictatorial powers, arguing that the task of the League was propaganda, which could now be carried on quite publicly. Therefore the newspaper took over the leadership of the 'Party'. It was a 'movement', and there was no thought of any organization. There was a workers' association in Cologne, but it considered Marx's democratic policy 'opportunistic'. Out of about three hundred Communists who had returned from Paris to all parts of Germany, only very few were of any political importance in the eyes of the newspaper. All prerequisites were lacking for a mass political organization of the extreme left; the masses themselves were lacking. So the newspaper was a lonely outpost of a social democracy, such as France had known but which was hitherto unknown in Germany.

The newspaper followed the events of the German revolution from this perspective, commented on its importance in the sphere of international politics, and decisively indicated the path by which the liberal bourgeoisie ought to complete the revolution. By June however a part of the ground conquered by the revolution had already been lost. Whilst the Frankfurt National Assembly debated about a constitution in a vacuum, the decrees of the Prussian National Assembly were already bound by the agreement of the Crown. The Prussian governments of Camphausen–Hansemann, Hansemann, Pfuël and Brandenburg marked various stages of counter-revolution. Thus all the newspaper's burning appeals were passionate indictments of the liberal bourgeoisie which had no idea how to create a revolution. Of the Frankfurt Assembly the paper said: 'German unity, like the German Constitution, can only emerge as the result of a movement in which both the inner conflicts and the war with the East are brought to resolution. The definitive process of constitution cannot be achieved by decree; it coincides with the movement that we must pass through.'

The paper explained to the Hansemann cabinet:

> The domination of the bourgeoisie cannot be reached by a compromise with the feudal powers. In this task, which is full of contradiction and consists of a dual battle, we constantly find that bourgeois domination has first to be

Marx as chief editor

> created only to see its existence outflanked by reaction in the feudal and absolutist sense – and then defeated by it. The bourgeoisie can never attain its own domination, without first acquiring the whole nation as allies, without becoming more or less democratic.

At the end of June the Paris workmen were defeated in several days of street-fighting – an event which hastened the counter-revolution in all European countries. But the newspaper saw this as a prelude to the real revolution 'because events have taken the place of phrases'. The paper then took the workers' side more decisively than was possible in France. The editorial board did not seem to be troubled by the fact that now the last shareholders slipped away. Victims of the National Guard and the militia, who fell in the rising, would be looked after by the State, and the forces of reaction would glorify them as 'protectors of order'. 'But the common people are torn by hunger, reviled by the press, abandoned by the doctors, abused by honest folk as thieves, incendiaries, and galley-slaves; their wives and children are plunged into even deeper misery, and their finest spirits are deported overseas. To bind the laurel round their grim brows, that is the privilege, indeed the right of the democratic press.'

From the very first the newspaper had campaigned for a revolutionary war against Russia. For a short time this was under consideration in Paris and Berlin and perhaps, if there had been an international front of liberalism, it might have saved the revolutionary movements. But there was no such front; in each country the liberals were intent on their own purposes. In the meantime the Tsar had offered assistance to the Prussian Court in putting down the revolution – assistance which proved so effective in overthrowing Hungary. For Marx and Engels, as for many liberals, Russia was the bulwark of reaction in Europe and an obstacle to a new order of freedom. To struggle against Russia was the alpha and omega of their foreign policy: 'War with Russia is the only war for revolutionary Germany; this is the only war that will cleanse the misdeeds of the past, the only war in which we can take heart and defeat our own autocrats. In this war, as befits a nation shaking off the chains of a long and indolent slavery, Germany can purchase the spread of civilization by sacrificing her sons, and make herself free within by gaining freedom without.'

With great determination the newspaper leapt to the defence of all oppressed nations, Italians, Hungarians, Poles; it was particularly passionate about the Poles, since they had to take an active part in the war of revolution. Prussia gave the Poles self-government; but when they were preparing a blow against Russia they were violently struck down. In a number of articles the newspaper attacked the government's Polish policy; for it saw clearly that the betrayal of Poland meant the betrayal of the revolution and the abandonment of the revolutionary war. It attacked just as fiercely the so-called democratic Pan-Slavism, as expressed in Bakunin's *Appeal to the Slavs*: 'All Pan-Slavists set nationality – that is to say, imaginary universal-Slav nationality – *before* revolution.' Since the Austrian Slavs favoured counter-revolution, the answer to Bakunin's demand that they should be given their independence was as follows: 'It is out of the question. In answer to these sentimental phrases about brotherhood, spoken in the name of the most counter-revolutionary nations in Europe, we say: for Germans, hatred of Russia must always be the primary revolutionary quality.... Now we know where the enemies of revolution are concentrated: in Russia and the Slav lands of Austria. Mere phrases and plans for a vague democratic future in these countries are not going to prevent us from treating our enemies as enemies' (Engels). If the newspaper denied that there was any historical future for the small Slav nations, this was partly because they were only tools of Tsarist policy. But it was also because, though the historical necessities of great nations could not be achieved without violence and ruthlessness, it was only their success that enabled the small nations to participate in a historical development that would otherwise have been impossible for them.

The newspaper was firmly convinced that the revolution would flare up again. In September it remarked that the crisis in the Prussian government might well prove the starting-point of a new revolution. And when Pfuël was appointed, the newspaper forecast that the revolutionary crisis would soon mature. At the beginning of November, when there was a suppression of the rebellion by Viennese workers and students (intended to help Hungary by hindering the retreat of the troops), the newspaper made a declaration of revolutionary terrorism:

> The annihilating counter-stroke of the June revolution will be struck in Paris. After the triumph of the 'Red Republic' in Paris, the armies will be spewed out over the frontiers from the interior of the countries, and the real force of the contending parties will be clearly revealed. Then we shall think of June and October, and we shall cry: *Vae Victis!* The pointless slaughters of June and October, the very cannibalism of counter-revolution, will convince the nations that there is only one way of shortening the murderous death-pangs of the old society and the bloody birth-pangs of the new society. There is only one way of simplifying them and concentrating them – namely, by revolutionary terrorism.

After the Berlin National Assembly had resolved in November to refuse to grant supplies, the newspaper organized opposition which was not to remain merely passive. The Cologne jurors acquitted Marx of a charge of calling for armed resistance, after he had pleaded the people's right to resist in response to the government's counter-revolutionary manoeuvres. At the New Year he announced: 'A revolutionary rising of the French working class, and world war – that is the agenda for 1849.'

England becomes the rock on which all revolutionary movements will founder – England, the country that 'makes whole nations into its proletariat', spanning the world and ruling the world-market: a continental revolution that did not include England would be a storm in a tea-cup. Old England could only be overthrown by a world war; but any European

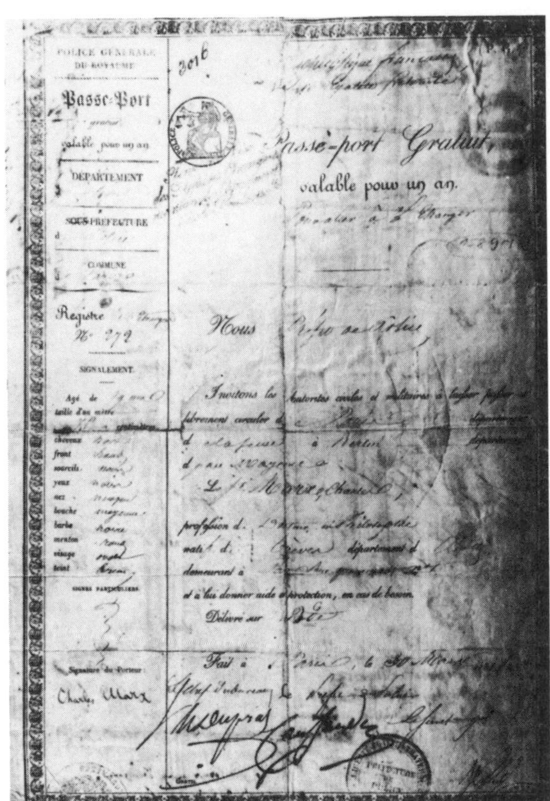
Passe-Port
DÉPARTEMENT
COMMUNE
Registre
SIGNALEMENT
Passe-port Gratuit,
valable pour un an.
Nous
Charles Marx

Marx's passport, Paris 1848

war that involved England would necessarily become a world war. Only when the Chartists were at the head of the British Government would social revolution leave the sphere of utopia and enter the sphere of reality.

It is noteworthy however that, even during the swift advance of counter-revolution, Marx and his friends still thought they could be effective in the ranks of democracy. During the Commemoration of the Berlin Rising of 18 March, the editors proposed toasts to the proletarian revolution, to the Paris victims of June, and to the Red Republic. It was not till the middle of April that they announced their withdrawal from the Democratic Union, as containing too many heterogeneous elements for useful work to be possible; instead they linked up with Born's Brotherhood of Workers. Hitherto the newspaper had generally paid little attention to the workers' movement, because, in accordance with its main policy, it first wanted to work for the victory of the liberal bourgeoisie.

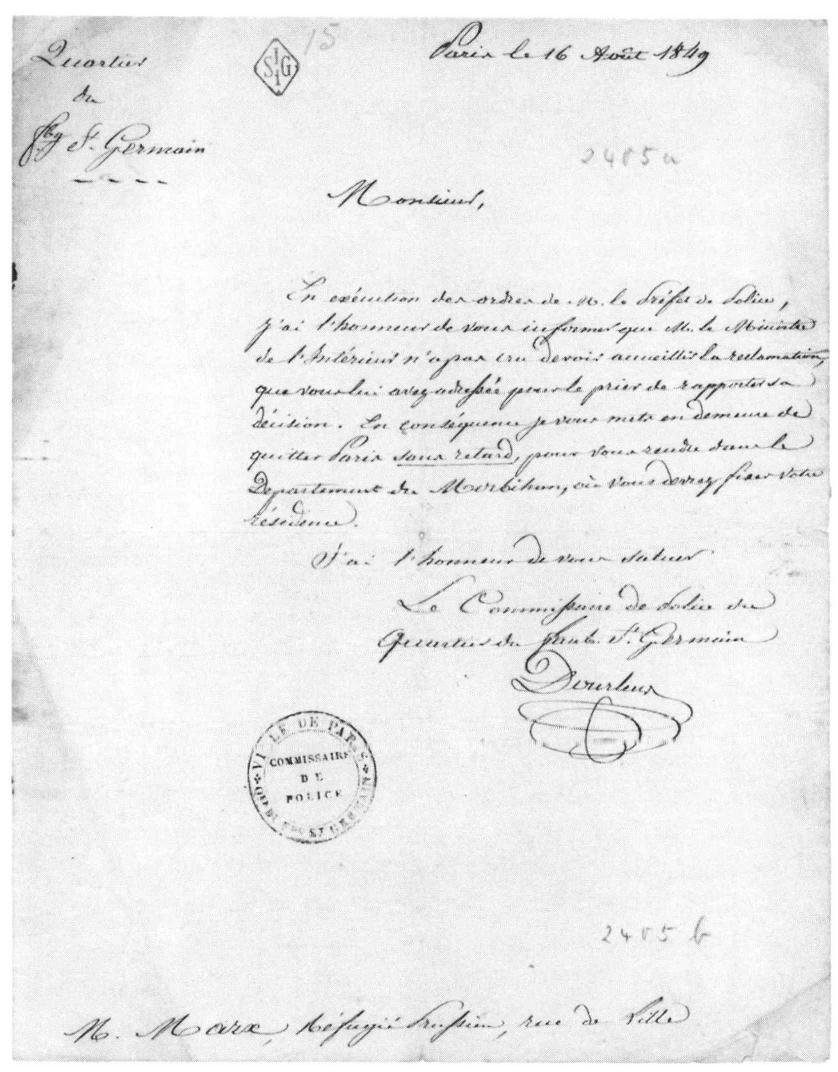

Quartier du Fbg St Germain

Paris le 16 Août 1849

Monsieur,

En exécution des ordres de M. le Préfet de Police, j'ai l'honneur de vous informer que M. le Ministre de l'Intérieur n'a pas cru devoir accueillir la réclamation que vous lui avez adressée pour le prier de rapporter sa décision. En conséquence je vous mets en demeure de quitter Paris sans retard, pour vous rendre dans le Département du Morbihan, où vous devrez fixer votre résidence.

J'ai l'honneur de vous saluer

Le Commissaire de Police du Quartier du Faub. St Germain

Dourlens

Ville de Paris — Commissaire de Police — Fg St Germain

M. Marx, réfugié Prussien, rue de Lille

Marx's expulsion order from Paris in 1849

Now it published Marx's essays on *Wage Labour and Capital*, in order to educate the workers. From the very first the liberal bourgeois were in no doubts about the character of the newspaper; they had understood both the *Communist Manifesto* and the newspaper itself. Hence the danger of Communism must have seemed much greater to the bourgeoisie than it actually was, which increased their fears about collaboration.

The counter-revolution had now become so strong that it could no longer tolerate a paper like the *Neue Rheinische Zeitung*. The simplest way of eliminating it seemed to be to expel Marx as a stateless person. This occurred on 16 May 1849.

The newspaper could bid farewell to its readers with some self-respect. Its policy had been consistent from its very first number; it had demanded *a social republic* and declared the necessity of *revolutionary terrorism*. It reminded its readers of its New Year forecast and proclaimed: 'A revolutionary army in the East, composed of fighters of all nationalities, now stands facing Old Europe embattled in the Russian Army; from Paris comes the menace of the "Red Republic"!'

As the tide of revolution ebbed, the attitude of the newspaper became more and more radical (though there was a certain inner logic in this). In view of the final success of the counter-revolution, this would have been almost impossible to understand, if it had not been that Marx and his friends really believed that the revolution would continue. It was not till over a year later that they realized the defeat was a final one, and that there was absolutely no more hope of the revolutionary democracy for which they believed themselves to be fighting.

In the summer of 1848 Charles Dana and Albert Brisbane visited Cologne, where they met Marx. They were, respectively, editor and correspondent of the *New York Daily Tribune*, a paper for which Marx later became the European correspondent. Brisbane remembered Marx as follows: 'At that time he was just beginning to make his mark. He was a man in his thirties, of a stocky burly build, with a distinguished face and thick black hair. His features bore an expression of great energy, and behind his moderate reserve one could detect the passionate fire of a bold spirit.'

7

FIRST YEARS IN LONDON – THE SLEEPLESS NIGHT OF EXILE

Marx had to leave Prussia within twenty-four hours. In South Germany he said goodbye to Engels, who took part in the Baden campaign, and then went on to Paris. The fact that he arrived there as 'Representative of the Democratic Central Committee' no longer meant very much. In his difficult material straits (the last receipts from the newspaper had exactly covered the debts) he probably received a loan from his mother; moreover friends in the Rhineland, including Lassalle, gave him some support. Frau Marx deposited her silver trinkets at the Frankfurt pawnshop and went with the children and Helene Demuth to Trier; in July 1849 the family was able to reunite in Paris. For the time being they were not very hard hit; it was, they thought, only one of those changes of fortune that are unavoidable in a revolutionary epoch. But when the government ordered Marx to go and live in Brittany, he refused to allow himself to be buried alive there, and went to England. It was his final departure from the Continent.

Marx arrived in London at the end of August. He planned to bring out the *Neue Rheinische Zeitung* as a monthly, until it might be possible to return to Germany and continue with the newspaper. He had no doubts about the success of the periodical; but during the course of 1850 only five numbers of the 'Political and Economic Review' appeared. It was not easy to distribute the magazine, which was printed in Hamburg, although it contained such brilliant contributions as Marx's *Class Struggles in France*, as well as Engels's account of the campaign for a Reich Constitution, and his study of the Peasant War. It was only with difficulty that the two friends managed to secure a few subscriptions, and there was a deficit from the first number onwards. Understandable as Jenny Marx's complaint against Weydemeyer was, it was not really justified:

> The only thing my husband could ask from those who had received many ideas, much assistance and support from him, was that they should show more businesslike energy and more participation in his review. I am proud enough and bold enough to assert this. It is the very least that one owes him.

She marvelled that her husband managed to raise himself above the shocking worries of daily life 'with all his energy, and all the calm, clear consciousness of his being'. His friends in Germany had daily proof that the revolution was over, and this had caused their spirits to sink.

Although Marx's view of history centred on the revolution, which all his writings to date had shown to be altogether necessary, and although at the time of the rebellion itself he had passed as the undisputed authority of the extreme left, he now had to force himself to accept the fact that the revolution was over. With ruthless honesty he accepted this conclusion, which must have affected him most deeply as a thinker and party-politician. During the next three years, old ideas were reviewed, the political organization was finally liquidated, and thus Marx's activities took on an entirely different character. The way in which he (together with Engels) worked out the further development can be followed in the various numbers of his review.

In *The Class Struggles in France*, Marx analysed the history of the revolution as a complex interaction between the main stream of economic development with its class-formations, on the one hand, and the stream of more superficial events at a party-political level, on the other. In the first chapter, he still considered it a possibility that revolution might be renewed in France. He thought that the June defeat had at last created the social conditions in which France might once again take the revolutionary initiative:

> Only when it was dipped in the blood of the June insurgents did the tricolour, become the flag of European Revolution – the Red Flag. And we cry out: 'The Revolution is dead! Long live the Revolution!'

But at the same time, in the journal's monthly news-survey, mention was made of the discovery of the Californian gold-deposits as being a fact that might be 'even more important than the February Revolution'. Gold would flow throughout America and the Pacific Coast, and thereby world-trade would change its course. Hence the only chance left for European countries of not lapsing into second-rate nations lay 'in a social revolution. This must, while there is yet time, revolutionize the methods of production and commerce in accordance with the produc-

Ferdinand Lassalle

tion needs that arise out of modern productive forces'. It is true that here, according to the hoped-for pattern of revolution, cause and effect were reversed. In this way Marx – after noting the French counter-revolutionary development in the constitutional bourgeois republic, after the abolition of universal suffrage, and indeed chiefly as a result of studying the reports in *The Economist* – eventually arrived, in the last number of the journal, at a deeper understanding of the reasons why the revolution failed. The European revolutions were only possible as a result of the great English commercial crisis of 1847 and its effects on the continent of Europe. The wave of economic prosperity that set in in 1849 paralysed the revolutionary advance everywhere. This meant that an economic crisis was a prerequisite for revolution: the economic basis of society must be destroyed before a revolution in the political sphere could be possible.

> In this state of general prosperity ... there can be no question of any real revolution. Such a revolution is only possible at periods when there its opposition between two factors – between modern forces of production and bourgeois forms of production. The various squabbles which now divide the representatives of the different splinter-groups in the party of continental order ... are only possible because for the time being the basis of events is so secure and (though the forces of reaction do not know this) so *bourgeois*. In the face of this all reactionary attempts to stop bourgeois development will fail, as will any moral indignation and any enthusiastic proclamations by the democrats. A new revolution is only possible as the result of a new crisis. But one is as certain as the other.

The great democratic movement that France had known ever since the French Revolution no longer existed; it had now been replaced by the class-division into bourgeoisie and proletariat. Marx's political detachment from the democratic movement showed itself in his struggle against so-called *petty-bourgeois democracy*, whose inadequacies he compared with his own concept of the movement, once so strong throughout Europe, but which in Germany had played just as little real part in proletarian revolution as the Communist League had done. Even more important for Marx was his own relationship to politics, that is to say, chiefly to the Communist League. This developed parallel with his growing insight into the causes of the revolutionary failure.

Whilst, in the spring of 1849, Marx rejected Schapper's refounding of the Communist League in Cologne, he still thought it was possible to work in the ranks of democracy; so immediately on arriving in London he set about refounding it himself, ignoring Schapper who remained behind in Germany. The League and the Refugee Committee, which the socialist emigrants Marx, Engels, Willich, Bauer and Pfänder founded to support the refugees streaming into London, provided the theatre of activities. In a long circular from Marx's Central Committee of March 1850, the new revolution is announced as imminent, 'whether it will be produced by an independent rising of the French proletariat or by an invasion of the Holy Alliance against the revolutionary Babel'.

The tasks appointed for the proletariat in such a revolution are specified exactly. As against the democratic petty-bourgeois, who considered the revolution would be over once their restricted demands had been carried through, the workers must proclaim *permanent revolution*; they must no longer appear as an appendage of democracy, but must constitute themselves as 'an independent organization of the working-class party, both secret and public'. In order to be able to counter any treachery, the workers must be armed: 'The whole proletariat must at once be armed with rifles, carbines, cannon and ammunition.' The workers had always got to outbid the demands of the democrats:

> if the democrats apply for a moderate progressive tax, the workers will insist on a tax in which the scales rise so steeply that it will destroy large-scale capital; if the democrats require that State debts should be regulated, the workers will require the State to go bankrupt. The demands of the workers will always be adjusted to the concessions and standards of the democrats.... The German workers can at least be certain that the first act of this revolutionary drama will coincide with the victory of their own class in France, which will hasten their own victory.... Their battle-cry must be: Permanent Revolution!

These abstract tactics, suitable for a policy in a vacuum, soon showed their unreality. Of course illusions like those of the leaders were also harboured by those who had been particularly close to the enemy, as soldiers fighting for the revolution in Baden or elsewhere – people like Willich and Schapper and the workers attached to them. The difference between the emigrant groups was simply that Marx and his supporters were quicker to realize that the revolution was over, whereas the simple soldiers went on dreaming that it would continue. The squabbles between the groups have to be seen in the context laid down by Marx himself at a meeting of the Central Committee on 15 September 1848. Here the split became clear, but Marx softened it with certain remarks which form a parallel with his new insights formulated above, though they must have astonished the other group:

> The minority is substituting a dogmatic view for a critical one, and an idealistic view for a materialistic one. Instead of real events it is taking mere decision to be the driving-force of revolution. We say to the workers: You have got to go through fifteen, twenty or fifty years of civil war, not merely to alter the relationships but to change yourselves and make yourselves capable of political rule. But you on the other hand say: We must achieve power at once, or else we can simply lie down and go to sleep! Whereas we are drawing the particular attention of the German workers to the possible future of the German proletariat, you are grossly flattering the national sentiment and the class-prejudice of the German artisans, which is of course much more popular. Just as the democrats give the word 'Nation' a holy connotation, you do the same with the word 'Proletariat'.

It is not surprising that this was taken to be a right-about-turn and that it gave rise to serious disputes. Marx 'saved' the League by removing the Central Committee to Cologne. So in London there existed two conflicting groups, that of Marx and that of Willich and Schapper. The central points of the struggle were frequently obscured by the sordid aspects of refugee life.

Marx and Engels's sudden *volte-face* was not readily understood by their companions. Even English political circles dung more to the other group, which represented the majority of the refugees. Marx and Engels became increasingly isolated. On 11 February 1851 Marx wrote to Engels:

> Quite apart from that, I am pleased with the obvious and authentic isolation in which you and I now find ourselves. It altogether suits our attitude and our principles. The whole system of reciprocal concessions and putting up with half-truths, and the necessity of playing one's part in the absurdity of the Party with all those other idiots – that's all finished with now.

On 13 February Engels replied:

> At last we have another opportunity (the first one for a long while) of showing that we have no need of any popularity or any support from any party in any country whatsoever. We can show that our position is completely independent of all those shabby tricks.... If the time comes when those gentlemen need us, we shall be in a position to dictate our own terms.... How do people like us, who avoid official situations like the plague, fit into a 'Party'? After all, we spit on popularity, we should not know what to do with it if we got it; what use to us is a Party, i.e. a bunch of idiots who swear loyalty to us because they think we are just like themselves? Frankly, it will be no loss if we stop being the 'proper mouthpiece' of those narrow-minded dogs we have been thrown with over the last few years.... Just think of all the gossip there will be about you among that whole pack of emigrants, when you bring out your *Economics* ... ?

Marx and Engels were now at the nadir of their public effectiveness. Marx expressed his disgust with the German and French refugees as being 'Franco-German ruffians of the galleys and barracks'; and he called Harney 'that impressionist plebeian'. On hearing that former supporters in Germany were 'wild with anger' at them, Engels drew the bitter conclusion: '*Et puis* did we not have to fight for our position in Cologne in 1848? The red democrats, even the Communists, are never going to *love* us.'

For Marx this nadir coincided with the nadir of his private existence. At any event he immediately threw himself into the study of economics, and shut himself up in the British Museum where he usually worked during the day. In January 1851 his friend Pieper reported to Engels: 'Marx lives a very secluded existence. His only friends are John Stuart Mill and Lloyd. And if one approaches him one is greeted with economic expressions instead of salutations.'

The British Museum *c.* 1850

But the work frequently had to be interrupted, as one hears in April 1851:

> The worst of it is I am now suddenly interrupted in my studies in the library. I have got so far that I could be finished with the whole economic shit in five weeks. *Et cela fait*, I shall work out the economy at home and pitch into another science in the Museum. *Ça commence à m'ennuyer. Au fond* this science has made no progress since A. Smith and D. Ricardo, although so much has been done in the way of particular and often super-delicate investigations.

The scope of his studies increased as he realized what he still lacked:

> In addition, during my recent time at the Library, which I continue to visit, I have been swotting up chiefly technology and the history of the same, as well as agronomy, in order to get at least some sort of an idea of all this rubbish.

The Frankfurt publisher Löwenthal seems to have shown interest in Marx's work, but he wanted to start with the history of economics. In November 1851 Engels advised Marx to reply that

> it is no good upsetting your whole plan, that you have already begun working out the Critique, etc.... The Socialists would be the third volume, and the fourth would be the Critique (*ce qu'il en resterait*) and the famous 'positive' section, the part you really want. There are some difficulties in this arrangement, but it has the advantage that the secret is kept till the end. Only when the bourgeois has restrained his curiosity for three volumes it is revealed to him that we are not making Morrison Pills.... The main thing is that you should only reappear before the public with a great big book.... Then again it is absolutely necessary that you should break the spell caused by your long absence from the German book-market and by the recent cowardice of the booksellers.

In the poverty which during these years often reduced the family to proletarian levels, it was frequently impossible for Marx to work. The family, which now numbered six, lived in two rooms in Dean Street. Sometimes Marx could not go out of doors because his clothes were in the pawnshop; often he could not buy writing-paper and the family lacked vital necessities. At this time his daughter Francesca was born and died soon after. Frau Marx described these days in a letter to a woman-friend:

> The three children still alive lay beside us, and we wept for the little angel who rested near us, pale and cold. The dear child's death came at the time of our bitterest poverty. I ran to a French refugee who lived nearby and who had visited us shortly beforehand. He showed the greatest sympathy and gave me two pounds. With these we bought the little coffin in which my poor child now slumbers in peace. The child had no cradle when she came into the world, and this last little dwelling was long denied her.

Though Marx felt his withdrawal from politics harshly, it was made easier for him by certain disappointments which the year 1852 brought with it. During the first weeks, in great haste and amid considerable deprivation, he had dealt with Napoleon's *coup d'état*, in an article entitled *The Eighteenth Brumaire* for the review which Weydemeyer was planning in America. In this he wanted to show 'how the class-struggle in France created certain relationships and circumstances which enabled a mediocre and grotesque person to play the part of hero'. The same material that was dealt with in *The Class Struggles in France* is treated here as an independent historical process; but attention is given less to the development of events than to their inner logic. The style corresponds with this; by means of startling formulae Marx often manages to illuminate complex situations. The hopes he placed on publication were not fulfilled. After a considerable delay the issue of a small edition was only made possible because a worker sacrificed his dollar-savings. This

64 Dean Street, where Marx lived in London from May 1850 to October 1856

fiasco could not be blamed on Weydemeyer; it was all the more painful to Marx when Proudhon reccived 'several hundred thousand francs' for his work on the same subject.

Another disappointment was the trial of Communists in Cologne in October and November 1852, when seven defendants were sentenced to long periods of imprisonment. The trial was occasioned by the arrest of a delegate of the League in Leipzig in May 1851, but it was the result of a drive against the Communist League by the Prussian police. The government was anxious for a huge trial in order to demonstrate publicly the danger of the League's efforts, and so the political police employed all the disreputable methods which often figure so largely in their activities: the use of *agents provocateurs*, burglary in London, and the theft and falsification of documents. It was exhausting work for Marx to produce the material on which the defence could be based. Jenny Marx described this work in a letter to a friend: 'Full proofs of the falsification

Die Revolution,

Eine Zeitschrift in zwanglosen Heften.

Herausgegeben von

J. Weydemeyer.

Erstes Heft.

Der 18te Brumaire des Louis Napoleon

von

Karl Marx.

New-York.

Expedition: Deutsche Vereins Buchhandlung von Schmidt und Helmich.

William-Street Nr. 191.

1852.

Title-page of the magazine *Die Revolution*

had to be produced, and so my husband had to work all day long and into the night. Then everything had to be copied out six or eight times, and sent on to Germany by different routes, through France, Paris, etc., since all letters from here to Cologne are opened and intercepted.' In his *Revelations on the Communist Trial in Cologne*, Marx mercilessly castigated the behaviour of the police and the judicial procedure. Understandably, he expressed disappointment, in a letter to Engels in March 1853, that the pamphlet aroused no response in Germany:

> Aren't our people in Germany miserable slack dogs? We haven't had a word from them. They must have seen in the newspapers that there has been a pamphlet about their business. But they don't send a word. There's no reaction, no energy in them. They're just a lot of old women – *voilà tout*.

By doing this work Marx made amends for his carelessness in associating too closely with Colonel Bangya, an Austro-Prussian spy. For the latter Marx wrote a pamphlet against the representatives of petty-bourgeois democracy, under the title *The Great Men of Exile*; this was certainly not a glorious page in his literary activity. He was probably led to it by material necessity and by the twenty-five pound fee. He paid no attention to his friends' warnings against this man and relied too much on an ability to judge people which he did not possess. In present day literature there is practically no mention of this incident; it is one of the unsolved problems of research about Marx.

Marx could at last breathe a sigh of relief when he was able to close this chapter by formally dissolving the Communist League.

8

THE WRETCHEDNESS OF EXISTENCE

Marx's correspondence with Engels shows how the wretchedness of existence (which is the name he gave to his domestic misery) weighed heavily on him for several decades. Once in 1842, when apologising to Ruge for not having been able to send certain contributions he had promised, he made reference to 'the most unpleasant family controversies.... I cannot possibly burden you with an account of these private trifles. It really is a good thing that public troubles make it impossible for a man of character to be irritated by private affairs.'

Entirely concerned with the 'general welfare', it was easy for him to ignore his private misfortune. But in London this burst upon him with such fury that he could not maintain his stoic attitude. Certainly he had no shortage of complaints, since they appeared in an endless stream; and it is wonderful to see how from such complaints he can often turn to a factual statement about important problems. But it is certain that wretchedness hit this proud and sensitive man particularly hard, and left profound traces in his personality, his character and his work. It has often been asked why Marx was unable to complete his masterpiece *Capital*, to which he devoted more than three decades of his life, and it has been thought that the reason lay in theoretical difficulties. But the circumstances of the author's life make it rather seem miraculous that he was able to complete so much.

In most biographies this phase of his life, since it cannot be avoided, is touched upon lightly, and the misery serves only as an occasion for remarking that Marx ignored it with heroism. But we must not content ourselves with this. Does a man not become greater if we know the personal and material misery in which he was placed, and the difficulties under which he had to live and work? For Marx wretchedness was threefold: illness, continual lack of money, and family difficulties.

Marx's wife with their daughter Jenny, around 1854

After 1849 Marx suffered from complaints of the liver and gall from which he was never afterwards free.* The attacks usually came on in the spring and became more serious as the years passed. Often they were accompanied by headaches, inflammation of the eyes and more serious neuralgia in the head. In addition there were rheumatic pains; Marx himself sometimes complained of paralysis. In 1877 a nervous disorder appeared, which was even more serious than the liver complaint; and the doctor said he believed that the whole illness was really of a nervous nature. One consequence of the illness was protracted insomnia, which Marx fought with narcotics. The illness, which was hereditary in Marx's family, was aggravated by excessive work, particularly at night; he was accustomed to study during the day and write at night. It was made even worse by faulty diet: Marx was fond of highly seasoned dishes, smoked

* Marx's illnesses are described here on the basis of F. Regnault, 'Les maladies de Karl Marx' in *Revue anthropologique* (Paris, 1933), XLIII, 293 ff.

fish, caviare and pickled cucumbers, none of which are good for liver patients. Moreover he liked wine and liqueurs. Since he came from the Moselle he preferred wine; but he also drank beer, which he was often forbidden to have. If he gave up alcohol it was never for very long. He smoked an enormous amount, and since he usually had no money, it was usually bad-quality cigars. At each attack of the illness he was forbidden to smoke; but he only gave up for a few days. After 1863 Marx began to complain a lot about boils. These are very frequent with liver patients and may be due to the same causes. Several times the ailment began in October and reached its peak in January. The abscesses, which led to suppuration of the glands, were so bad that Marx could neither sit nor walk nor remain upright. After 1855 Marx often also got catarrh, which in the last years of his life led to tuberculosis of the lungs; the cause of death was 'cachexy as a result of consumption'. Tuberculosis also killed Edgar (nicknamed 'Musch'), whose death in March 1855 was a severe blow for the family. Jenny Longuet too probably died of it in January 1883; and even Jenny Marx was infected, having probably been disposed towards it by a similar kind of life. Though tuberculosis may well have been a hereditary ailment in the family, Marx was particularly susceptible to it through his long suffering. Repeated convalescence at English coastal resorts and on the Continent, besides what amounted to continuous attention by a doctor, only brought transitory relief to his sufferings.

Medicine tells us that in liver patients one often finds excessive intellectual activity and that they are unable to switch off their thoughts. It is known that Marx himself, when out for a walk, would brood and argue with himself, and that at night he found it hard to go to sleep. The character of the patient shows a strong irritability; he is impatient, irascible and dissatisfied, critical of everything and his mood is uneven. In Marx too the illness emphasized certain traits in his character. He argued cuttingly, his biting satire did not shrink at insults, and his expressions could be rude and cruel. Though in general Marx had a blind faith in his closest friends, nevertheless he himself complained that he was sometimes too mistrustful and unjust even towards them. His verdicts, not only about enemies but even about friends, were sometimes so harsh that even less sensitive people would take offence. There must have been very few whom he did not criticize like this – perhaps Bebel or Sorge. Not even Engels was an exception.

Undoubtedly all Marx's sufferings were made worse by psychological pressure and continuous lack of money. He gave more to society than he

Karl and Jenny Marx at the end of the 1850s

received from it. Paradoxically, when today any page with his writing on it would cost hundreds of pounds, he was never able to earn enough to keep his family. The fact that he was able to exist at all during the three decades in London was only due to Engels. Whatever the latter could spare he sent to Marx. Although it was a stroke of luck for him that his father owned a factory in Manchester, which he could join as a commercial traveller, his father still kept him very short. So at first he could only send a pound or two at a time; later the sums became larger, indeed sometimes he took on risky financial operations to help his friend. When Engels became a partner in the firm, Marx was able to live without anxiety. And when Engels retired and lived in London as a rich man, from January 1869, he set aside for Marx a yearly income of seven thousand marks which often had to be increased. In the twenties, the Marx–Engels Institute compiled a list of all payments that could be checked from the correspondence, and published something on the subject (in the same year in which its Director Riazanov fell into disfavour); the total must have come to a hundred and fifty thousand marks or more. But the details of the amounts are not important; nor the fact that Marx did not have to beg for the money, and that the incidents were treated in a purely businesslike way.

What was more important was that Marx's financial distress could not be overcome with money. There were times at which he received unexpectedly large sums; but they ran through his and his wife's fingers. Each of these windfalls only caused the living-standard of the household (though there was only enough to maintain it at a modest level) to become more stylish; thereafter the old distress recurred in a more serious form. When Jenny Marx inherited five thousand marks in 1856 on the death of her uncle and her mother, the family was at last able to leave the poor quarter in the autumn of that year and rent a house at 9 (now 46) Grafton Terrace in Kentish Town, North London. Engels was obliged to contribute even for the furnishing of this, and soon the Marxes were very hard up again. In January 1857 Marx wrote:

> I have absolutely no idea what I shall do next, and now I am in an even more desperate situation than I was five years ago. I thought I had already swallowed the ultimate filth. *Mais non*. And the worst of it is that this crisis is not temporary. I cannot see how I shall get out of it.

In March 1857 'everything possible' had already been pawned: 'everything in the house is in such a state that my head is buzzing too much for me to write. The situation is disgusting.' In May 1861 Marx, in great

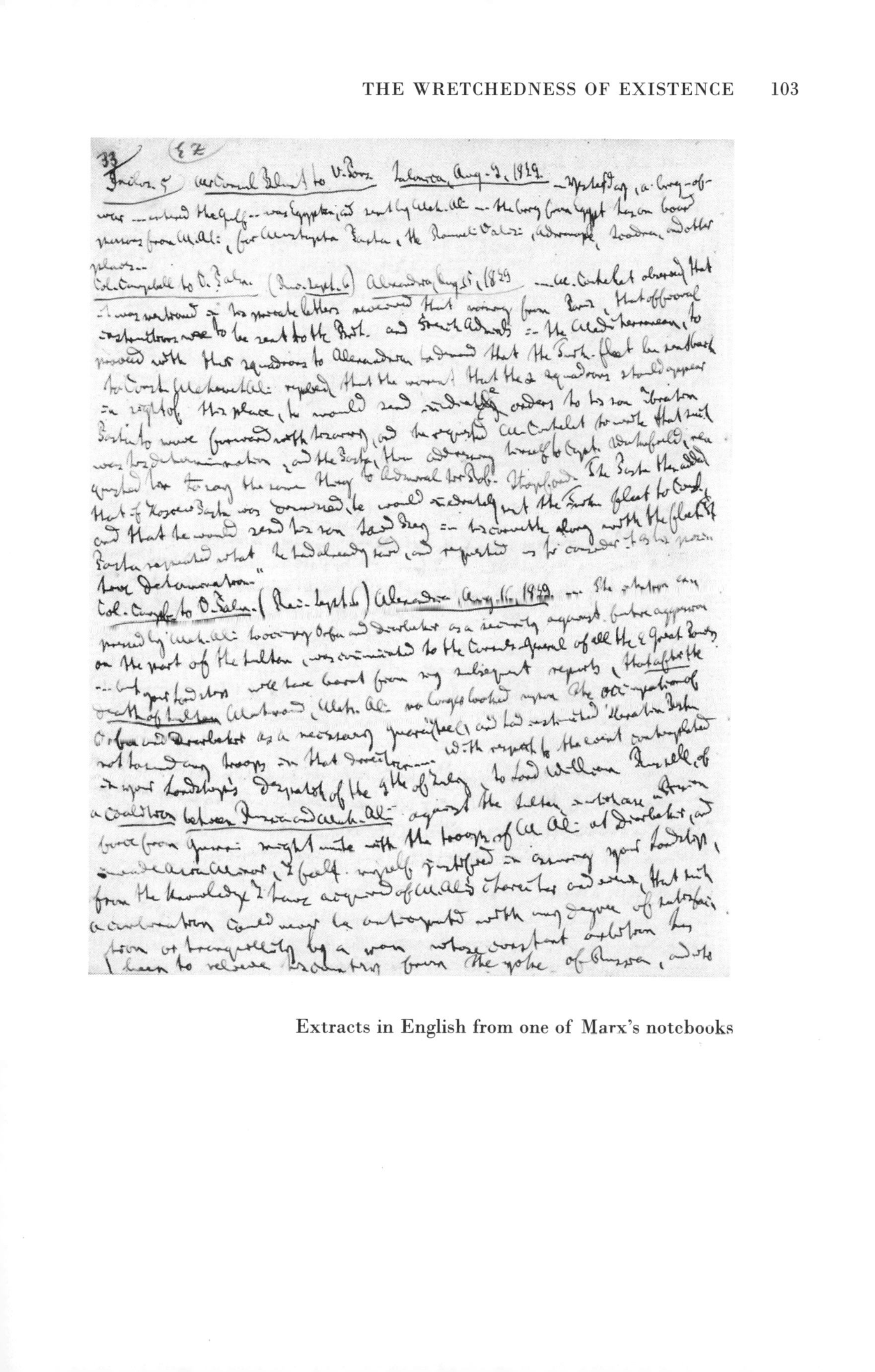

Extracts in English from one of Marx's notebooks

need, was able to get three thousand marks from his uncle, Philips, in Holland, and he managed to increase this by loans from a cousin of Philips, from Lassalle, from Ludmilla Assing, whom he met at Lassalle's, and from a German cousin of Engels. But the next month he had to ask Engels for forty marks, to pay taxes. In August 1862 he contrived to get a loan from Lassalle; but in the same month he wrote: 'If only I knew how to start some kind of business! My dear friend, all theory is dismal, and only business flourishes. Unfortunately I have learnt this too late.' Similarly:

> Every day my wife tells me she wishes she and the children were dead and buried. And really I cannot argue with her. For the humiliations, torments and terrors that have to be gone through in this situation are really indescribable.... I pity the poor children all the more because this has happened in the 'Exhibition season', when all their friends are enjoying themselves, while they are only terrified in case someone should visit us and see the filth.

In the summer of 1864 Marx received about thirty thousand marks. Of this about fourteen thousand marks was his inheritance from his mother; and the rest came to him as principal heir of Wilhelm Wolff, a friend who died in Manchester. Since just before this the distress of the family had reached a new peak, this freed him from a frightful burden. Marx permitted himself to move into a larger house, 1 Modena Villas, Maitland Park Road, also – like Grafton Terrace – in Kentish Town. But exactly a year later, in May 1865, he was obliged to return to the pawnshop. On 31 July he was writing to Engels:

> You cannot be surprised at this if you consider, firstly, that during the whole time I have been unable to earn a single farthing, and secondly, that merely to pay off my debts and furnish the house cost me nearly £500. I have kept account of this penny by penny ('as to this item') because it seemed to me astonishing how the money disappeared.... Altogether I am living above my means, and besides this year we have been living better than usual. But it is the only way in which the children (quite apart from all they have suffered and for which one could at least make it up to them for a short time) can find friends and relationships that will ensure them a future. I think you yourself will see that, even simply from a business angle, a purely proletarian set up would not be right here, though this might be all very well if my wife and I were alone or if the girls were young.

During the following year he was

> forced to borrow small sums here and there in London, just as in my worst times as a refugee – and this among a very restricted and indigent circle – merely to make the most necessary payments. On the other hand the

9 (now 46) Grafton Terrace, Kentish Town, where Marx lived from October 1856 until March 1864

> tradesmen are menacing; some of them have cut off our credit and threatened to sue. These matters are all the more serious since Lafargue is continually in the house and the real state of things has to be carefully hidden from him.... I know very well that you have done everything in your power and even more. But I simply must think of something. Is it not possible to get a loan or some other kind of arrangement?

These complaints about financial straits go on continuously throughout the years. Help is urgently needed for everything: rent, gas, light, rates, all kinds of food, school bills for the children, doctor's bills, etc.

But what must have been the effect on Marx of this life-long misery? He had once had the gift of behaving as if it did not affect him directly. As early as 1852 he wrote to his friend:

> You will have seen from my letters that, as usual when I am right in the shit myself and not merely hearing about it from a distance, I show complete indifference. Anyway, *que faire*? My house is a hospital and the crisis

> is so disrupting that it requires all my attention.... The atmosphere is very disturbed: my wife is ill, Jennychen is ill, and Lenchen has a kind of nervous fever. I couldn't and can't call the doctor, because I have no money for medicine. For eight or ten days I have managed to feed the family on bread and potatoes, but it is still doubtful whether I can get hold of any today.... I have written no articles for Dana because I had not a penny to go and read the newspapers.... Besides there is the baker, milkman, greengrocer, and old butcher's bills. How can I deal with all this devilish filth? And then finally, during the last eight or ten days, I managed to borrow a few shillings and pence which were absolutely necessary if we were to avoid giving up the ghost....

The persistent pressure must have broken down even Marx's 'indifference'. When Engels's mistress Mary Burns died at the beginning of 1863, Marx replied to this news with a couple of lines and immediately went on to describe his own troubles in great detail:

> If I don't get a larger sum, our household here can scarcely survive another two weeks. It is abominably egotistical of me to tell you of these horrors just at the moment. But the treatment is homeopathic. One trouble cures another. And, after all, what am I to do? In the whole of London there is not a single man to whom I can speak my heart freely, and in my own house I play the silent Stoic in order to counter outbreaks from the other side.... If only, instead of Mary, my mother, who anyhow is now full of physical infirmities and has lived a fair span of life.... You see what curious ideas can come into the head of 'civilized' people under the pressure of certain conditions.

After a few days Engels replied: 'You will not be surprised that this time my own misfortune and your frosty reply made it quite impossible for me to answer you before. All my friends, including Philistine acquaintances, have shown me on this occasion, which was bound to touch me very closely, more friendship and sympathy than I could expect. And you chose this moment to advertise your coolness! So be it!'

Marx's frank letter of apology made Engels rejoice that he had not at the same time lost his oldest and best friend. Marx wrote: 'In such circumstances, I can generally save myself only by cynicism. What made me specially mad was the fact that my wife believed I had not told you the full truth.' With particular reference to his wife he welcomed Engels's remarks:

> For we must put an end to the present situation – a process of being roasted over a slow fire, in which head and heart are consumed and valuable time is lost while we and the children have to keep up false appearances. The three weeks we have just gone through have at last caused my wife to consider seriously a proposal I made some time ago. In spite of all its

Engels, Marx and Marx's daughters Jenny, Laura and Eleanor in the mid 1860s

> drawbacks it is not only our only escape but is preferable to the life we have lived for the last three years (especially the last). It will also restore our self-esteem....

He wanted to have himself declared bankrupt, break up his household and arrange to live modestly. Engels prevented it from coming to this.

But we are still left with this cynicism which, increasingly throughout the years, always permeated all Marx's statements about people and events. What Engels called 'coolness' and Marxism calls 'objectification' may really have been the cynicism with which he viewed all events. It

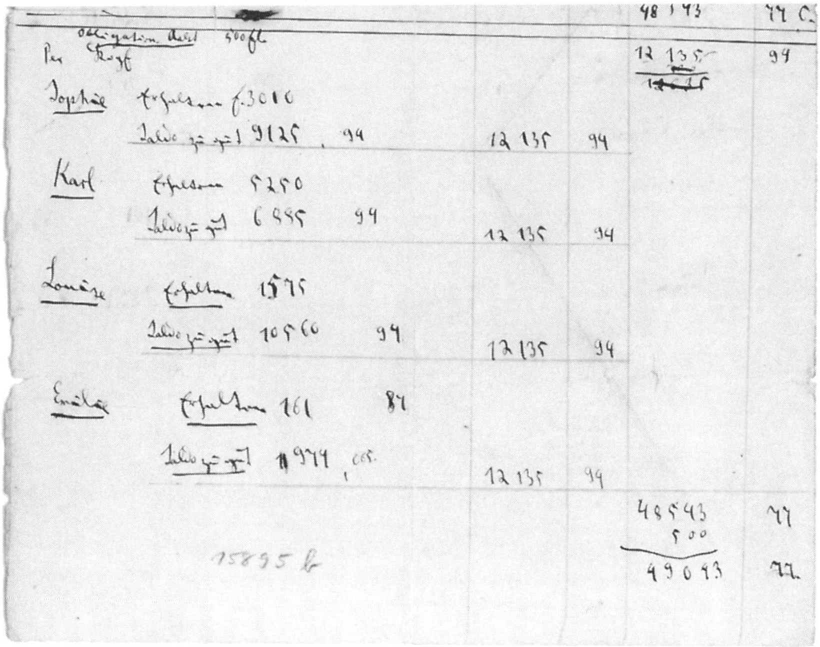

Marx's accounts of his mother's legacy to her children

was a kind of blunting of the feeling. In the summer of 1861 Marx visited his mother for two days and reported to Engels:

> There is no hope of any cash from my mother. She is rapidly approaching her end. But she has destroyed a number of promissory notes which I gave her earlier. That was one quite pleasant result of the two days that I spent with her....

And in December 1863 when his mother died he wrote:

> Two hours ago a telegram arrived to say that my mother is dead. Fate needed to take one member of the family. I already had one foot in the grave. In the circumstances I am needed more than the old woman. I have to go to Trier about the inheritance.... So I must ask you to send *by return* enough money for me to travel to Trier *immediately*....

In order to avoid having to state the real significance of poverty to Marx it has been usual to describe him as a bohemian. But it was precisely because Marx and his wife were *not* bohemians that poverty took on such a special importance for them. They did not have that happy gift of being able to squander money and then live for a time

Helene Demuth, who kept house for the Marx family for many years

without any money at all. Their whole conception and way of life was much more bourgeois, and for this very reason bourgeois poverty hit them particularly hard. It was not merely that Jenny Marx wanted to keep up false appearances; Marx himself liked to give visitors, and especially foreigners, the impression that he was living in comfortable bourgeois circumstances. If he wrote to the uncle in Holland who paid him his mother's legacy and said that he had won four hundred pounds speculating on the Stock Exchange, he did this to impress the banker uncle; and he was able to carry off this imaginary gain because his uncle

Eleanor Marx

knew nothing about the simultaneous legacy from Wolff. At the same time he hid from Engels the amount of his mother's legacy in order to give some plausibility to the speed with which the legacy from Wolff was vanishing. Marx himself said that he had to pay for this struggle to keep up false appearances with a loss in self-esteem. Moreover the amount of petty cheating entailed by the continual hunt for money (the necessary 'diplomacy and managing', as Jenny Marx calls it), damaged his self-respect. It was not only his relationship towards Lassalle and Kugelmann, for example, that was influenced; his relationship with Engels too was not free from it. The lifelong dependence on Engels must have weighed on Marx and his wife. Laura Lafargue destroyed the letters of her parents because they talked damagingly about Engels; and the few surviving letters confirm this fact.

Jenny Marx paid for this exhausting life with the progressive shattering of her nerves. Marx's complaints about poverty are accompanied by

Jenny and Laura Marx

complaints about the hysterical outbursts and eccentric fits of his wife; he mentions her dangerous 'nervous conditions'. As early as 1851 he says:

> At home everything is constantly in a state of siege, streams of tears exasperate me for whole nights at a time and make me completely desperate.... I pity my wife. The chief burden falls on her, and *au fond* she is right.... All the same you must remember that by nature I am *très peu endurant* and *quelque peu dur*, so that from time to time I lose patience.

These complaints continue. Later on any unfavourable piece of financial news from Engels produced 'a kind of paroxysm' in Jenny Marx.

And as if this domestic misery was not enough, the marriage relationship too was disturbed by a personal conflict, probably at the beginning of the sixties. Around 1900 all the socialist leaders knew that Marx was the father of Frederick (Freddy) Demuth, the son of Helene Demuth. But nothing could be said about it, partly because the fact itself, by the bourgeois moral standards of the time, was objectionable to those leaders, and partly because it did not fit the heroic and idyllic mould in which an idol of the masses should be cast. So all traces of this son were expunged, and it was only chance that prevented the destruction of a letter from Louise Freyberger-Kautsky to August Bebel, which tells us about it.* She writes:

> I know from General himself that Freddy Demuth is Marx's son. Tussy went on at me so, that I asked the old man straight out. General was very astonished that Tussy clung to her opinion so obstinately. And he told me that if necessary I was to give the lie to the gossip that he disowned his son. You will remember that I told you about it long before General's death.
>
> Moreover this fact that Frederick Demuth was the son of Karl Marx and Helene Demuth, was again confirmed by General a few days before his death in a statement to Mr Moore, who then went to Tussy at Orpington and told her. Tussy maintained that General was lying and that he himself had always admitted he was the father. Moore came back from Orpington and questioned General again closely. But the old man stuck to his statement that Freddy was Marx's son, and said to Moore: 'Tussy wants to make an idol of her father.'
>
> On Sunday, that is to say the day before he died, General wrote it down himself for Tussy on the slate, and Tussy came out so shattered that she forgot all about her hatred of me and wept bitterly on my shoulder.
>
> General gave us (i.e. Mr Moore, Ludwig and myself) permission to make use of the information only if he should be accused of treating Freddy shabbily. He said he would not want his name slandered, especially as it could no longer do anyone any good. By taking Marx's part he had saved him from a serious domestic conflict. Apart from ourselves and Mr Moore and Marx's children (I think Laura knew about the story even though perhaps she had not heard it exactly), the only others that knew that Marx had a son were Lessner and Pfänder. After the Freddy letters had been published, Lessner said to me: 'Of course Freddy is Tussy's brother, we knew all about it, but we could never find out where the child was brought up.'
>
> Freddy looks comically like Marx and, with that really Jewish face and thick black hair, it was really only blind prejudice that could see in him any likeness to General. I have seen the letter that Marx wrote to General in Manchester at that time (of course General was not yet living in London

* The letter is dated 2 September 1898. Only the passages dealing with the son are quoted. Louise Freyberger-Kautsky was the first wife of Karl Kautsky, and after the death of Helene Demuth in 1890 she came to Engels's house as housekeeper and secretary. Her husband was Engels's family doctor, and they lived with him. The writer of the letter was in a special position of trust with regard to Engels and Bebel. 'General' is well-known to have been the nickname of Engels; 'Tussy' was the name for Marx's youngest daughter, Eleanor.

then); but I believe General destroyed this letter, like so many others they exchanged.

That is all I know about the matter. Freddy has never found out, either from his mother or from General, who his father really is....

I am just reading over again the few lines you wrote me about the question. Marx was continually aware of the possibility of divorce, since his wife was frantically jealous. He did not love the child, and the scandal would have been too great if he had dared to do anything for him....

Needless to say, in this (as in the whole matter of his poverty) the question is not one of guilt. On the contrary, we must only ask: Did this son have any special significance for Marx? When his short-lived daughter Francesca was born in 1851, he told Engels: 'My wife has been delivered, unfortunately of a girl and not a boy.' And in 1855 he wrote to tell Engels about the birth of Eleanor: 'yesterday morning, between six and seven o'clock, my wife gave birth to a *bona fide* traveller – unfortunately of the "sex" *par excellence*. If it had been a male child, the thing would have been better.' In the same year his only son Edgar died, and he felt the death as a terrible blow of fate. But – this other son he did not love, as has been said; he could do nothing for him!

Marx and his wife were bound to be particularly affected by this incident precisely because their actions and thoughts were so thoroughly bourgeois. They could never think of Engels's companion (who was not legally married to him) as his 'wife', and in letters they always mentioned her in inverted commas. Moreover, as the correspondence shows, they observed the marriage-relationships of others with great subtlety. Perhaps they were really mollified by the way in which Engels played the part of a 'father'. But how else could one view the relationship but as yet another attempt to maintain false appearances?

Marx does not seem any smaller as a result of it; just as Dickens, that pattern of bourgeois respectability, loses nothing when we learn of his amorous double life; and just as Beethoven is not diminished when we know that he had a daughter by one of his admirers. Heaven protect us from small-mindedness! And Marx too becomes greater when we discern the conflicts that surrounded him, which would have destroyed weaker personalities far more quickly.

9

JOURNALISM AND CONTEMPORARY HISTORY

For a whole decade, from 1851 to 1862, Marx worked on contemporary history as a journalist. The work brought him little pleasure, for he was no journalist by nature. After only a year he complained to Engels:

> This continual scribbling for the newspapers bores me. It takes up a lot of time, everything goes to waste and there's nothing to show for it. For all the talk about independence one is tied to the newspaper and its public, especially if one gets paid cash as I do. Pure scientific work is something completely different.

And later: 'It is really loathsome to have to think oneself lucky that a filthy rag like that takes one on.'

His journalistic work at this time includes several hundred articles, of which a considerable number must of course be ascribed to Engels. In particular Engels's essays on military and strategic questions were very highly valued; Marx often sought his collaboration and seldom in vain, for Engels wrote briskly. The most important paper that took Marx's contributions was the *New York Tribune*, for which he (together with other journalists) acted as European Correspondent during these ten years. It was the largest American newspaper, leftwing liberal in tone; it opposed slavery and demanded protective tariffs for American industry. At the same time it had a socialist, Fourierist tinge. Marx owed his connection with the newspaper to a recommendation from Dana, whom he had met in Cologne. For a time he occasionally worked also for the *Neue Oder-Zeitung* in Breslau in 1855, for David Urquhart's *Free Press* in 1855–6, for Ernest Jones's late-Chartist *People's Paper*, and for the *Wiener Presse* in 1861-2.

For Marx journalism was a necessity since it did at least bring him some income on which he could rely. However even this was not quite

Marx in 1880

certain, for his articles were paid piecemeal, and the *New York Tribune* (like the *Wiener Presse* later) did not print all his contributions by any means. His articles were mostly aimed at American taste. Marx could not be surprised that his criticisms of English economics were taken as criticisms of Free Trade. The editors often used his articles as anonymous leaders if they could get credit thereby. After 1855 his articles were no longer signed, for he had demanded that either his name should be given always or else not at all. The interest shown by Americans in Marx's work fluctuated with their interest in European affairs. It was strong in time of war; it fell off when their own affairs seemed to them more important; and it disappeared entirely when the Civil War took all their attention. But after 1855 the articles dealing principally with Russian questions tended to be seriously altered and modified, because the influence of a Russian assistant on the editorial board awakened some sympathy for Russia. Thus, for example, fifteen articles by Engels about Pan-Slavism were left unprinted.

Marx's articles and reports are of varying quality. Often they were drafted reluctantly on the basis of other newspapers or the news of the day which the journalist could not really afford to ignore. Often, and above all where it is a question of a series of articles, they are very fundamental essays which are based on detailed study and analyse the political and social history of different countries. Whereas Marx's earlier style had tended to be philosophic and abstract, with strong echoes of Hegel, this was now relaxed by journalistic work; since he was now usually dealing with concrete matters that could not be dealt with abstractly, his style became more lively and colourful. Marx is by no means always wanting to provide proofs for the correctness of his view of history; that would have led to a pedantic and dogmatic tone which would scarcely have been tolerable in a newspaper. He also knows the value of descriptive and individual touches (what he used to call the 'petty-bourgeois attitude') as suiting the American taste, and he asks Engels to pay a lot of attention to this.

The great importance of this journalism for Marx was that it forced him to study day-to-day politics, not only English domestic and economic politics but also all events on the international scene, so that his horizon was immensely enlarged. Whereas by 1848 he had already acquired the criteria for viewing the basis of economic events, he now learnt to take a more living view of things. There is much in his essays of social and economic criticism that we find appearing again in the material for *Capital*. And a number of the articles are models of social criticism, such as that on the Duchess of Sutherland, who proclaimed her sympathy with the emancipation of slaves, whereas her ancestors had expropriated English agricultural labourers on a large scale.

During this decade international politics were dominated by the oriental question, by the Russo-Turkish War and the Crimean War of 1854–5, the Spanish Revolution of 1854, England's relations with Russia, England's Indian policy and the Indian Mutiny of 1857, the European crisis and the Italian War of 1859. All these events were followed in detail by Marx. Here we are concerned largely with the day-to-day history of party-politics and the diplomatic chessboard, and not with the basic long-term history of society, its economic foundations and political needs. Consequently he does not use historical dialectic – the choppy seas of day-to-day history make this impossible; rather he is purely informative. Indeed frequently Marx even takes a certain relish in portraying particular situations, intrigues, and personal traits. There was a lot of historical material in actions and ideas which could not be linked directly with the social process.

It goes without saying that Marx devoted particular attention to crises. Thus he was expecting a crisis in 1851, and then again in 1852, 1853 and 1855; when the commercial crisis of 1857 started in America and seized on England and the Continent, he was in a fever of expectation. On 13 November he wrote to Engels:

> Although I myself am in financial distress, I have never since 1849 felt so cosy as during this outbreak. You can calm Lupus too by telling him that in a big article in the *Tribune* (now that the whole statement is before us, and using the table of discount-rates for 1848–54) I have proved that normally the crisis would have occurred two years earlier. Even the delays can now be explained so rationally that Hegel himself would have been pleased to recognise the 'concept' in 'the world's empirical conflict between ultimate interests'.

Engels felt the same; his reply is dated 15 November:

> I feel the same as you. Since the whole thing collapsed in New York I have been unable to find any peace in Jersey, and I feel an enormous faith in this general breakdown. The bourgeois filth of the last seven years had still been clinging to me to a certain extent, but now it's all washed away and I feel a different man. The crisis will do me as much good physically as a bathe in the sea, I can feel that already. In 1848 we were saying: 'Now our time is coming'. And it did come in a certain sense, but this time it's coming completely. It makes my military studies so much more practical. I am at

> once hurling myself into studying the organization and tactics of the Prussian, Austrian, Bavarian and French Armies, and also riding, i.e. foxhunting, which is the real training.

In addition to the crisis he carefully followed the wars, and not merely because these interested the American readers. Marx considered that war was really a form of revolution, which 'seizes on the periphery of the social body and strikes inwards: it puts a nation to the test. Just as a mummy will fall to pieces in an instant if it is exposed to the atmosphere, so war gives the death-blow to all institutions that are no longer alive.' But many events which aroused great expectations were no more than 'superficial destruction'.

Whereas at one time Marx and Engels had concentrated their attention on Germany, this had long ceased to be the case. In foreign policy they had even given up the idea of European democracy. For that attitude, foreign policy had been determined by the antagonism between France (as personifying revolution) and absolutist Russia, and the fight between these two powers had been the historical task of the nineteenth century. But now this view had been somewhat altered. Russia was still the bulwark of reaction, and the yardstick for measuring the politics of the powers was still their attitude towards Russia. Marx now believed that 'Anglo-Russian thraldom' was the key to an understanding of international politics. From his study of the blue books, the diplomatic reports and parliamentary proceedings, he thought he had discovered that, since the time of Peter the Great, there had been a secret understanding between the English and Russian governments, and that even Palmerston was a paid agent of Russian policy. These subtle investigations took Marx into the somewhat dubious company of the English diplomat David Urquhart, a fanatical enemy of Russia and friend of Turkey, for whose newspaper, the *Free Press* of Sheffield and London, he wrote a series of articles on 'The History of the Secret Diplomacy of the Eighteenth Century'. Some of these, including two essays on Palmerston, were published separately as pamphlets in a large edition.

It has recently been assumed that Marx and Engels's attitude towards Russia was influenced by Urquhart, and that in this they 'followed the lines of the old state-politics in a very "un-marxist" manner'. In fact, they had always held to the anti-Russian approach of European democracy, and this was slow to alter. It was only after the Emancipation of the Serfs in 1861 that they believed they could detect an internal development in Russia, which they now watched attentively. Hostility against all things Russian blazed up again at the suppression of the Polish rebellion of 1863, and then once again during the dispute with Bakunin. When a revolutionary movement got going in Russia, and especially when it adopted terrorist methods in the fight against Tsarism, their views on Russia underwent a definitive change. Marx and Engels occupied themselves intensively with Russian economic problems, and at the same time became less interested in an independent Poland as a bulwark against Russia. At the beginning of the eighties they began to believe that revolution was going to come from the East, and not from the West. It could only be a bourgeois revolution; but it would overthrow Tsarism and would permit Europe to carry through the social revolution successfully. The change of view about Russia was determined by political expectations, and it was facilitated by an intensive study of the internal development in Russia.

One of the advantages of this period, during which Marx followed current affairs as a journalist, was the more realistic evaluation of events that he acquired. In the inaugural address of the International he pointed out that the emancipation of the working class could not be achieved 'with a foreign policy which pursues frivolous ends, appeals to national prejudices, and squanders the property and blood of the people in predatory wars'. One of the first duties of the working class was to

> master the secrets of international politics. It must keep an eye on the diplomatic acts of the various governments; when necessary, it must work against them with every available means; when it cannot anticipate them it must unite in simultaneous protests against them; and it must seek to validate those simple laws of morality and justice, which are supposed to govern the relations between private persons, as the supreme laws of intercourse between nations....

A wealth of material on the emigration during the decade following on 1848 is to be found in Marx's very detailed, indeed too detailed, polemic *Herr Vogt*; he published this in 1860 as a reply to the calumnies of the natural scientist and 'Regent of the Reich' of 1849. Vogt had accused Marx of organizing conspiracies of German workers with the knowledge of the police, and had said that Marx was the head of a gang of blackmailers in London. Marx accused the Berlin *Nationalzeitung* of printing these calumnies. When his prosecution failed, Marx had to spend a whole year collecting material to disprove the slanderous statements. The various developments are only of interest to the specialist. The work shows Marx's polemic at the height of its effectiveness. His

Ferdinand Freiligrath

assertion that Vogt had been paid to advocate Louis Napoleon's policy was confirmed after the collapse of the Second Empire: in August 1859 Vogt had received forty thousand francs.

Marx's friendly relations with Ferdinand Freiligrath received a shock which led to a breach, for the poet refused to allow himself to be drawn into this affair. Marx reminded him of their joint revolutionary background (here the chief interest is their notion of 'the Party') when he wrote on 23 February 1860:

> We are both conscious that, each in our own way, neglecting all private interests and acting from the purest motives, we have for years waved the banner of the '*classe la plus laborieuse et la plus miserable*' high over the heads of the Philistines. So I should hold it something of a sin against history if we were to part for the sake of trifles – which are all due to misunderstandings.

Freiligrath replied on 28 February:

> When, towards the end of 1852, the League was dissolved as a result of the Cologne trial, I severed all links that bound me to the Party as such. All that was left was my personal relationship to *you*, my friend and political comrade.... My nature, and that of any poet, needs freedom! Even the Party is a kind of cage and one can sing better out of it than in, even when one is singing *for* the Party. I was a poet of Revolution and the Proletariat long before I became a member of the League or joined the editorial board of the *Neue Rheinische Zeitung*! So I want to continue standing on my own feet, I want to belong only to myself and have sole responsibility for myself!

On 29 February Marx wrote:

> Since 1852 I have had *nothing* to do with 'Party' in the sense you mean in your letter. If you are a *poet*, I am a *critic*, and I had quite enough experience from 1849 to 1852. The League, like the Société des Saisons in Paris or like a hundred other societies, was only one episode in the history of the Party, which sprang naturally from the soil of modern society. [I have] ... tried to explain the mistake you make in thinking that, by 'Party', I mean a 'League' that has been dead for eight years, or an editorial board that was dissolved twelve years ago. By Party I mean the Party in the grand historical sense.

10

LASSALLE: MARX'S DISLIKE OF GERMAN SOCIAL DEMOCRACY

After the expectations aroused by the crisis of 1857 had been disappointed, Marx was anxious (as he wrote to Lassalle) to have some years of

> superficial peace. In any event it is a good time for scientific enterprises; and finally, after the experiences of the last ten years, contempt for the masses and for individuals has grown so great in every rational being that *odi profanum vulgus et arceo* has almost become a maxim of life. But these are simply Philistine sentiments that will all be swept away by the first storm.

This storm was heralded in about 1860, when the workers in England and on the Continent began to bestir themselves. Approaches made by the delegations of French and German workmen, who came to London in 1862 for the World Exhibition, had awakened a desire among the English labour leaders for some form of international association. At the end of 1864 this led to the founding of the Working Men's International Association, the so-called First International. Eighteen months before, Lassalle had begun a noisy agitation in Germany; he was not going to put up with the founding of the International. Whereas in this Marx was soon to play the leading role, the development of the German working men's party at this time took place entirely without any help from him. He and Engels were excluded from any active political work, and they followed developments with unconcealed dislike and distrust. Their correspondence gives quite sufficient information about this. It is also known that later on, when they advised the German Party on particular questions (and this advice was not by any means always followed), they had difficulty in freeing themselves from this mistrust. Engels really only lost it a few years before his death, under the influence of August Bebel and the electoral victory of the German Social Democrats, which vindicated

ADDRESS

AND

PROVISIONAL RULES

OF THE

INTERNATIONAL WORKING MEN'S ASSOCIATION,

ESTABLISHED SEPTEMBER 28, 1864,

AT A PUBLIC MEETING HELD AT ST. MARTIN'S HALL, LONG ACRE, LONDON.

PRICE ONE PENNY.

PRINTED BY THE WESTMINSTER PRINTING COMPANY,
56, AND 132, DRURY LANE.

Title-page of the Address of the First International

Bebel's tactics as 'the right ones'. The view that Marx and Engels were the real leaders of social democracy and drew up its policy is one that belongs entirely to the sphere of legend. This mistrust was due entirely to Lassalle. There are three reasons why he was important for Marx: the relationship with him presents one of the most complex psychological problems in Marx's life; it always determined his attitude towards social democracy; and it shows the extent to which the political and personal aspects in Marx were interwoven.

The two men became acquainted in 1848, and visits to Cologne and Düsseldorf soon created a close friendship. Towards 1860 Lassalle certainly recognized Marx as the head of the 'Party', while Marx was impressed by Lassalle's energy and intelligence. Whereas Lassalle was always honourable in his friendship towards Marx and moreover believed in Marx's friendship for him, this soon gave place to feelings of mistrust which were probably either aroused or fostered by Engels. In the eyes of Engels, Lassalle was the 'Jew from the Slav border', the '*parvenu*' in whom he did not like the 'mixture of frivolity and sentimentality, of Judaism and mock chivalry'. As soon as his suspicions were aroused Marx was open to any insinuations. Even quite obvious slanders on Lassalle that reached Marx were accepted by him as the truth without any investigation, and he would preserve them for future use. In this way they became estranged. But this did not prevent Marx (using cunning diplomacy with Lassalle) from making frequent use of his services in financial matters or for securing introductions. Many of the most unfriendly statements in his correspondence with Engels are aimed at Lassalle. The reader of the correspondence between Marx and Lassalle discovers with astonishment how skilfully Marx succeeded in concealing his enmity and how naïvely Lassalle continued to believe in Marx's friendship. The dislike was not founded on any political differences. It existed long before 1859, when during the Italian War Lassalle advocated a view that differed from that of Marx and Engels. Marx, fully convinced that he and Engels represented the true party line, conceived this to be a flagrant breach of party discipline. Political differences might perhaps have increased the dislike; but for Marx, Lassalle was quite antipathetic enough already. No less egocentric than himself, his style of life was provocatively eccentric. He had everything that Marx lacked. He was wealthy and could keep up a large house in Berlin, a fact that Marx was able to discover for himself on a visit there in the spring of 1861. His great scientific works were highly praised, whereas Marx could make

August Bebel

no progress with his. As a brilliant speaker and pamphleteer he took the masses by storm, whereas the masses knew nothing about Marx. Whilst the latter wore himself out with journalism, Lassalle expressed an arrogant disapproval of this; he preferred to devote himself only to 'important works', and told Marx about his plans for some of these. In addition his extravagant style of life made a particularly unpleasant impression at times when Marx was suffering especially from poverty.

Marx considered that these works were 'the bungling efforts of a schoolboy', and it was unbearable to him that the 'schoolboy' went ahead by himself and even presumed to give Marx advice like a schoolmaster. It is understandable that Marx was anything but pleased when Lassalle began his agitation. As ill-luck had it, Lassalle's *Programme for the Workers* reached Marx just at the time when there was a serious disagreement between him and Engels after the death of Mary Burns. He could see nothing in the work but 'a poor vulgarization of the *Communist Manifesto*', and said: 'The fellow clearly thinks that he is going to take over our stock.' On 9 April 1863 he was writing to Engels:

> Itzig [one of the milder nicknames for Lassalle] has already published two pamphlets about his case again, which, fortunately, he has *not* sent me. On

> the other hand he sent me the day before yesterday his open letter in answer to the Workers' Central Committee for the Leipzig Workers' (for this read Louts') Congress. His attitude – very important, flinging about phrases borrowed from us – is quite that of the future workers' dictator.

And on 21 April Engels wrote:

> We have got our opponents in the right position and the Lout has become conscious and so transferred himself to the ranks of the petty-bourgeois democracy. But to regard these chaps as representatives of the proletariat! It takes Itzig to do that.

And Engels again on 20 May:

> These stories of Lassalle's and the scandal they are creating in Germany are beginning to get unpleasant. It is high time that you finished your book, if only to give us some different kind of standing-ground again. Besides it is a good thing that we shall be able once more to work against the bourgeoisie, it is only disastrous that it will let Itzig consolidate his position....

Marx on 22 June:

> As soon as I get some peace I shall devote myself to the fair-copy of my pig of a book, which I shall go to Germany and peddle myself.... For this time Itzig is forcing us not to hide our light under a bushel.

And again on 6 July:

> Itzig has sent me a new pamphlet, his speech in Frankfurt-am-Main. Since I am already spending ten hours a day studying economics I can hardly be expected to waste my leisure reading this schoolboy exercise. So for the moment it's filed away. In my free time I'm going on with differential and integral calculus.

On 15 August Marx notes that Lassalle :

> reveals himself as a first-former who with the most revolting and bombastic old wives' chatter trumpets abroad – as his latest discovery – principles which (ten times better) we were already distributing as small change among our partisans twenty years ago. The same Itzig otherwise also collects in his manure factory the party excrements we dropped twenty years ago, with which world history is to be fertilized.

This was the tone in which their verdicts were given. It was only after Lassalle's death that a more conciliatory note appeared in their letters. On 4 September 1864 Engels wrote: 'What rejoicing will reign among the factory owners and the Progressive swine – Lassalle was after all the only chap they were afraid of in Germany itself.' And on 7 September Marx replied:

Friedrich Engels

> After all he was still one of the old guard and the enemy of our enemies. And then the thing came as such a surprise that it is hard to believe such a noisy, 'stirring', 'pushing' person is now as dead as a mouse and has got to keep his mouth shut 'altogether'.

The basis of the accusations against Lassalle was the ever-recurring charge that he had plagiarized Marx's earlier writings and used them as a foundation on which to build a party. This aspect of the question is cautiously weighed by Gustav Mayer, Engels's biographer, whose verdict springs from a sound knowledge of the relationship: 'They [Marx and Engels] looked upon it as a kind of unfair competition, all the more so as in this case the difference between scientific discovery and political action (which they were usually well aware of) was to a great extent obscured.' They considered it a cardinal error in Lassalle's tactics that he pursued a one-sided struggle against the liberal bourgeoisie, a policy that was bound to lead to a risky game with Bismarck. Lassalle could reply that it was a question of detaching the workers from the ranks of the progressive party, and that the workers wanted a specifically *working-class* party; from this point of view the other side had the appearance of 'a reactionary mass'. And Lassalle's supporters were in fact the most progressive representatives of the proletariat at that time; in the form that Marx and Engels desired, it did not exist at all. Lassalle no longer considered that the strategy of the *Communist Manifesto* (i.e. to support the bourgeoisie until it had attained power) was appropriate; a revolutionary initiative could no longer be expected from the German bourgeoisie. It was not till about 1890 that Engels, under the influence of Bebel, surrendered his ideas of 1848 and adopted this point of view. Marx and Engels also objected to the term 'Social Democrat'; it was 'a pig of a name', but quite good enough for this movement. They themselves used to call themselves Communists, to avoid getting confused with the many blends of socialist. Since the disbanding of the Communist League they called themselves Socialists.

To account for Marx's rejection of Lassalle, it has been remarked that Marx was not concerned principally with founding a working men's party, but much more with revolution. Yet on this very point it would be impossible to misjudge the situation more seriously than Marx and Engels did. They outdid one another in illusory expectations of revolution. In February 1863, after the debate in the Prussian Second Chamber about the Polish Rebellion, Marx said: 'We shall soon have revolution'. In June Engels thought that the troops, distributed half on the Polish frontier

Wilhelm Liebknecht

and half on the Rhine, could well leave Berlin free and then revolution might occur. In April 1866 Marx predicted that the Hohenzollerns and the Hapsburgs would set Germany back fifty or a hundred years through civil war, if no revolution broke out. A Prussian hegemony in Germany seemed unthinkable to them; they felt revolution was much more likely. Three weeks before the battle of Königgrätz, Engels believed that Prussia was certain to be defeated, and prophesied that then there would be a rebellion of the militia: 'I believe that within a fortnight it will start in Prussia. If they let this opportunity go by and the people put up with it, then I think we can just say goodbye to all our revolutionary ideas and devote ourselves to theory....' The lesson of Königgrätz did not last very long. In November 1867 Engels was expecting revolution in France any day; then Germany and England would be drawn in, and the social question would then be on the agenda at once throughout the whole of Europe.

German Social Democrats were constantly reproaching the two friends in London for the fact that they entirely misinterpreted the situation in Germany. Liebknecht gave a very good answer when they disapproved of his policy: he said that in the sixties he had a choice between plunging into the torrent that rushed past him, or else of standing quietly philosophizing on the bank. It was clear that the second alternative was intended to describe the attitude of the two Londoners. Here we see clearly the two different planes – scientific research and political action on the one hand, history of philosophy and politics on the other. Any blending and confounding of the two was bound to prevent any understanding being reached in the everlasting discussions between the so-called Marxists and the so-called Revisionists; not only that, but it would be altogether fatal for Social Democrat policy. This is what Liebknecht meant by saying: 'It would be the greatest misfortune for the movement if the theoreticians were to determine its policy.' It also explains why he concealed from the Party Marx's *Critique of the Gotha Programme* of 1875. His aim was to unite the two German parties, the one tending more towards Lassalle and the one tending more towards Marx; it was no concern of his that certain concepts should be formulated with the greatest dogmatic clarity. Liebknecht had no sympathy for the fact that Marx was violently opposed to Lassalle's 'iron law of wages' and to the latter's productive guilds that were to be formed with the aid of the State. For Liebknecht knew that the facts about the Law of Wages (originally formulated by Malthus and Ricardo) were to be found in the *Communist Manifesto*, and that it was only after the death of Lassalle that Marx formulated his Theory of Surplus Value. Moreover Liebknecht also knew that, in the Inaugural Address and in the Statutes of the First International, Marx had granted those productive guilds an important place among the demands of the workers, and this only a few months after Lassalle's death. Even such a sympathetic critic as Karl Korsch had considerable difficulty (during his Communist period) in explaining the violence of Marx's attacks on these points. Nor did Liebknecht think it at all necessary to the workers' movement that, after its organization and effectiveness within the framework of the 'present-day State' had been acknowledged, this present-day State (whose reality was drastically demonstrated each day) should be made out to be a mere 'fiction', and one that would vanish with the disappearance of its roots in bourgeois society.

Marx mistakenly believed that, in bringing out this programme, the party leaders were committing 'a monstrous attack on the view that was

1 Modena Villas, Maitland Park Road (destroyed by bombing in the Second World War): the house where Marx lived from March 1864 until his death in 1884

current among the mass of the Party'; for at no time were his views by any means widely current. At the beginning of 1891 Engels succeeded in getting Marx's critique of the programme printed in the *Neue Zeit*, and thus achieved some belated satisfaction at the expense of Lassalle. It was another source of satisfaction that the Erfurt Programme of the same year drew upon some of the doctrines expressed in Marx's critique. But if one attempted to maintain that this Programme enabled Social Democracy to pursue a 'proper' Marxist policy, or if one were to think that a programme could guarantee a correct policy, then once again 'the difference between scientific discovery and political action would largely disappear'.

11

THE INTERNATIONAL – A LIFE AND DEATH STRUGGLE

During the Revolution of 1848 Marx's political activity was directed towards capturing an outpost: namely the outpost of revolutionary democracy which existed then in France, but which never existed in Germany, either then or later. The Working Men's International Association offered him new possibilities for political activity on a wider stage. The International owed its inception to the initiative of English and French working men; it was founded at a mass meeting in St Martin's Hall, London, on 28 September 1864. Marx was one of the thirty-two members of the committee that was supposed to draw up the statutes. And Marx was soon to become the principal brain in the central leadership of the association. Even though for years he scarcely appeared in public, and did not himself attend any of the congresses except the last, from the very beginning it was he who directed the General Council. He wrote the Programme which has become known as the Inaugural Address, he drew up manifestoes and resolutions for the congresses, he was Secretary for Germany, and he also carried on a great deal of correspondence for the organization.

Marx's course of action was very different from what it had been earlier on. The Communist League had been a secret propagandist society in which Marx enjoyed dictatorial powers. But the International was a union of independent (and jealously independent) organizations of working men in various different countries. Marx had no dictatorial powers; he was only one among a number of members on the General Council. It was always a question of convincing the other members. For the International contained many different currents of thought; there were supporters of Fourier, Cabet, Proudhon, Blanqui, Bakunin, Mazzini and Marx himself. There were all shades of opinion ranging from peaceful

1/

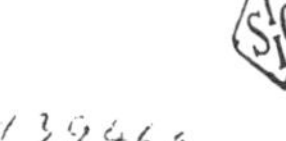

S.I.G.

Statuts

De l'Association Internationale des Travailleurs

Votés à la séance du Congrès du 5 September 1866.

13946 a

Considérant:

Que l'émancipation des travailleurs doit être l'œuvre des travailleurs eux-mêmes; que les efforts des travailleurs pour conquérir leur émancipation ne doivent pas tendre à constituer de nouveaux privilèges, mais à établir pour tous des droits et des devoirs égaux et anéantir toute domination de classe;

Que l'assujettissement économique du travailleur à l'accapareur des moyens du travail, c'est-à-dire des sources de la vie, est la cause première de la servitude dans toutes ses formes — misère sociale, dégradation mentale, soumission politique;

Que, pour cette raison, l'émancipation économique des travailleurs est le grand but auquel tout mouvement politique doit être subordonné comme moyen;

Que tous les efforts faits jusqu'ici ont échoué, faute de solidarité entre les ouvriers des diverses professions dans chaque pays, et d'une union fraternelle entre les travailleurs des diverses contrées;

Que l'émancipation du travail n'étant un problème ni local, ni national, mais social, embrasse tous les pays dans lesquels la vie moderne existe et nécessite pour sa solution leur concours théorique et pratique;

Que le mouvement qui reparaît parmi les ouvriers des pays les plus industrieux de l'Europe, en faisant naître de nouvelles espérances, donne un solennel avertissement de ne pas retomber dans les vieilles erreurs, mais de combiner immédiatement tous les efforts encore isolés;

Par ces raisons:

Le Congrès de l'Association Internationale des Travailleurs tenu à Genève du 3 au 8 septembre 1866, déclare que cette association, ainsi que toutes les sociétés ou individus y adhérant reconnaîtront la Vérité, la Justice, la Morale, comme la base de leur conduite envers tous les hommes, sans distinction de couleur, de croyance ou de nationalité.

Le Congrès considère comme un devoir de réclamer pour tous les droits d'homme et de citoyen. Pas de devoirs sans droits, pas de droits sans devoirs.

13946 b

First page of the *Statutes* of the First International

Utopian Socialists, to the Anarchists for whom the revolution was a matter of fighting on the barricades. There were English trade-union leaders, whose unions – the organizational mainstay of the International – were rooted in a section of society where the old professional pride of the guilds still lived on. There were the Germans, easily organized and disciplined, and also the inflammable revolutionaries of the Latin countries.

Marx's programme, which was unanimously accepted, had none of the tone of the *Communist Manifesto*, with its tinge of history of philosophy and its rousing call to revolution. It is true that it does say:

> The economic subjugation of the worker by those who have misappropriated the means of production (i.e. the sources of life) lies at the root of every form of serfdom. It is responsible for social poverty, spiritual atrophy and political dependence. Therefore the economic emancipation of the working class is the principal aim which every political movement should serve to further.

But with regard to events in England the path to emancipation is presented in a very unemotional manner. Whereas during the period of the industrial advance after 1848 the wealth of England had grown enormously, the working classes had become impoverished and apathy had seized on the masses. But since that time two events of great importance had occurred: the law prescribing a Ten-Hour Day, and the growth of the Co-operative Societies, particularly the producer co-operatives. This growth could not have been accomplished without state assistance, and to this end the working class was obliged to fight for political power and influence over the legislature. Hitherto the lack of an international association had condemned the efforts of the workers in the different countries to failure. Since they were continually menaced by the criminal foreign policies of governments (with their concealed threat of war), the workers were obliged to concern themselves with international politics.

Marx laid the foundations of this change in tone when he wrote to Engels on 4 November 1864:

> It was very difficult to frame the thing so that our view should appear in a form acceptable from the present standpoint of the workers' movement.... It will take time before the reawakened movement allows the old boldness of speech.

During the next six years Marx's political style remained as realistic as it was in the Inaugural Address. It was not until he wrote about the Paris Commune that the 'old boldness' reappeared. The varying character of the working class movement in the different countries precluded any other style. Moreover Marx was affected by his ten years' experience of journalism with the continuous observation of day-to-day politics it had entailed. And there was also much to be learnt from the success of Lassalle's agitation over the limited objectives of electoral suffrage and the Co-operatives. At the various congresses of the International (in London 1865, Geneva 1866, Lausanne 1867, Brussels 1868, and Basle 1869) subjects included the question of working hours, the labour of women and children, the trade unions, education, attitudes towards the State and towards political action, and so forth. In all these Marx was anxious (as he wrote to his friend Kugelmann) that one should confine oneself 'to those points which allow of immediate agreement and concerted action by the workers and give direct nourishment and impetus to the requirements of the class struggle and the organization of the workers into a class'. Marx took on a gigantic load of work on behalf of the International; he seldom failed to attend the weekly sessions of the General Council, and he engaged in continuous discussion in order to convince the other members. But it scarcely needs to be said that he did not view his position in the light of a secretary. He always believed that he was exerting a continuous influence on the General Council behind the scenes and that in fact he was really directing the whole organization. He was not mistaken when he told Engels on 11 September 1867:

> Things are moving. And in the next revolution, which is perhaps nearer than it appears, *we* (i.e. you and I) will have this powerful engine in our hands.... And without any financial means, moreover. With the intrigues of the Proudhonists in Paris, of Mazzini in Italy, of the jealous [trade-union leaders] Odger, Cremer and Potter in London, with the Schulze-Delitzschites and Lassalleans in Germany! We can be very well content! ...

It was not a need for personal power that drove Marx on, he was fighting on behalf of his ideas; but it was *his* ideas that were bound to win through in one way or another. During the early years it was the supporters of Proudhon who opposed his 'centralist and authoritarian' line. But the internal struggle only began to endanger the existence of the organization when Marx was opposed by the Russian anarchist Mikhail Bakunin; with his revolutionary temperament Bakunin exercised on those around him the same kind of suggestive influence that Marx did with his powerful intelligence. He had fought on the barricades in Dresden in 1849, he had been extradited and had escaped from exile in Siberia. This revolutionary past had given him the reputation of a 'Man of Action' of great personal courage; in tactical cunning he was a match for Marx. They had known each other since the time they spent in Paris. When Bakunin turned up in London in 1864, Marx said to Engels about him: 'Seeing him again after sixteen years, I find he is one of the few people who have gone forwards and not back.' In 1868 Marx sent him, as an 'old Hegelian', a copy of *Capital*. Bakunin always had the greatest respect for Marx's scientific work, even though he was sceptical of all 'scientific abstractions' and considered them dangerous, as presuming to dictate to reality. At Marx's invitation Bakunin also became a member of the International; he announced that he had joined in the following words: 'My Fatherland is now the International, of which you are the most important founder. So you see, my dear friend, that I am a pupil of yours, and proud to be one.'

Yet they were quite aware of the antagonism between them. Bakunin's supporters were mostly to be found in the International Alliance of Socialist Democracy, which was particularly strong in the Latin countries; at the Basle Congress there had already been an indecisive struggle for power between the two factions. About this Bakunin wrote to Alexander Herzen (after acknowledging Marx's great merits) that things might reach a point 'where I have to quarrel with him. Not of course attack him personally, but quarrel with him over a matter of principle, namely State Communism which is advocated so strongly by him and by the Germans and Englishmen whom he leads. That could be a life and death struggle.' Bakunin rejected Communism because it concentrated all power in the State and inevitably led to the centralization of property in the hands of the State. 'Whereas I desire the abolition of the State. I want to root out completely that principle of authority in the State by which men have always been enslaved, oppressed, exploited and humiliated.' He rejected all political action that did not directly promote the social revolution; even the International had got to concentrate exclusively on that.

It is difficult to decide whether it was these differences of principle, or whether it was individual preferences about organization that led to the 'life and death struggle'. One is inclined to view the latter as the main cause, all the more so since there was a certain stratum in Marx's ideas which sympathized with the Anarchist wish to abolish the State. At the end of *The Poverty of Philosophy*, and at the end of the second section of the *Communist Manifesto*, Marx did say that the public power (which was really the force of one class organized in order to suppress another) would lose its political character. At least in a letter dated 28

Mikhail Bakunin

January 1884, Engels drew the attention of Eduard Bernstein to these passages for use in the political agitation against the Anarchists, as a proof that Marx 'had proclaimed the abolition of the State, long before there were any Anarchists at all'. The difference here is that the abolition of the State only featured in Marx's philosophy of history at the point where 'in the course of development class-differences would have disappeared'; with Bakunin on the other hand, the State was to be abolished at the very outset of the revolution.

The decisive battle came at the Hague Congress in September 1872, about which Marx wrote to Kugelmann: 'At this Congress it will be a question of the very life or death of the International. And before I retire I will at least protect it from destruction.' Marx 'saved' the International (just as at one time he had saved the Communist League from the danger of Willich's majority) by moving the headquarters of the General Council to New York. This put an end to its existence in practice. Even before that, Bakunin and some of his followers had been expelled. Even among Marx's supporters there was widespread indignation about the fight against Bakunin, in which he personally was treated very unfairly, and it did Marx's reputation a lot of harm. After the Congress Jenny Marx (and here she was certainly speaking for her husband) wrote to Johann Philipp Becker about an article in the *Tagwacht*:

> What pleases me especially about what you have done, is that you have had the moral courage to treat things *personally*. Even our loyal working men have often had serious attacks of decency and objectivity, and then like real bourgeois they raised a cry of 'No personalities, nothing but facts and principles!' As if, when one is fighting against such people, there were any chance of making a distinction between persons and principles!

It was because Marx identified himself with his cause that he was able to fight for it so vehemently. Any fight for the cause was at the same time also a personal fight for him; but it meant that the cause took on certain personal features.

Just as in 1891 Engels enjoyed a certain satisfaction over Lassalle by publishing Marx's *Critique of the Gotha Programme*, so on this point too he attempted to vindicate the past. At the founding of the Second International in 1889, he urged Bebel to begin the work of the International at the point where the first had ended – namely with the fight against the Anarchists. Bebel showed no sympathy for this attitude, since these were no longer live issues.

In addition to this internal conflict there was a far more serious external attack on the International which took the form of persecution by various governments. This increased after Marx had claimed the rising of the Paris workmen, the Commune of 18 March to 28 May 1871, as a victory for the International. To be sure, in moving words Marx honoured the memory of the tens of thousands who, after heroically defending the beleaguered city, were slaughtered by the ferocious soldiery – just as once before, in the *Neue Rheinische Zeitung*, he had honoured the memory of the June victims. But his book *The Civil War in France*, written in English and published as a memorandum of the General Council, is the most characteristic example of Marx's understanding of events and the way in which he interpreted them for his political theory. In reality the Commune was the municipal government of Paris, the administration of this capital city that was besieged by the German armies and had been abandoned by the Government. A minority in it were socialists, but the majority were petty-bourgeois artisans and

Der

Bürgerkrieg in Frankreich.

Adresse des Generalraths

der

Internationalen Arbeiter-Assoziation

an

alle Mitglieder in Europa und den Vereinigten Staaten.

Separatabdruck aus dem Volksstaat.

Leipzig.

Verlag der Expedition des Volksstaat.

1871.

Title-page of the German edition of *The Civil War in France* intellectuals. The measures they carried through were the emergency measures necessary in a besieged city. The International, including the few supporters of Marx in France, took no part in the preparations for the rising and for some time they were in two minds whether to join it. Marx and Engels believed that a rebellion would only stand some chance of success after peace had been concluded; and they severely criticized the indecision of the municipal administration and the pointless political squabbling among the different factions. After the defeat Marx immediately asserted, with his 'old boldness of speech', that he and the General Council were solidly in favour of the insurgent workers. The glorification of the Commune, the creation of the whole myth of the Commune, re-emphasizing important arguments in the *Communist Manifesto*, is chiefly the work of Marx. This interpretation is confirmed by that great expert on the Commune, Georges Bourgin, when he says that it shows 'the revenge of one class against another. The everyday pettiness, the political squabbling of the government of the Paris Commune, was enacted against the backcloth of a great social drama, in which the audience of today are the sons and heirs of the actors of yesterday.'

Marx interpreted the municipal administration of the besieged city and its emergency measures in the following terms:

> Its true secret was this. It was essentially a working-class government, the produce of a struggle of the producing against the appropriating class, the political form at last discovered under which to work out the economic emancipation of labour. Except on this last condition, the Communal constitution would have been an impossibility and a delusion. The political rule of the producer cannot coexist with the perpetuation of his social slavery. The Commune was therefore to serve as a lever for uprooting the economical foundations upon which rests the existence of classes, and therefore of class rule.

In Marx's view the Commune was the particular form of government, the 'Dictatorship of the Proletariat', which would permit a transition to be made to the classless society. Later when Eduard Bernstein was in doubt about this, he asked Engels and received from him the following reply on 1 January 1884:

> The fact that in the *Civil War* the unconscious tendencies of the Commune are represented as being more or less deliberate plans, was quite justified in the circumstances, perhaps even inevitable. The Russians have, quite correctly, used this passage from the *Civil War* as an appendix to their translation of the *Manifesto*.

Page from the manuscript of the first chapter of the second volume of *Capital*

The idea that Marx did no more than take 'the unconscious tendencies' of the Commune and bring them to consciousness is a notion that is not supported by the historical facts. The distortion fitted his political theory. Although Engels was aware of the falseness of this theory of the Commune, he gave particular emphasis to Marx's mythological account when he published the new edition of the book in 1891.

Even Marx knew the truth, and he was himself capable of estimating the political importance of the Commune in a realistic manner. When the Dutch socialist Ferdinand Domela Nieuwenhuis asked him what measures a workers' government should take, if it came to power unexpectedly, Marx replied to him on 22 February 1881, evading and contradicting his own theory:

> Perhaps you will point to the Paris Commune; but apart from the fact that this was merely the rising of a town under exceptional conditions, the majority of the Commune was in no sense socialist, nor could it be. With a small amount of sound commonsense, however, they could have reached a compromise with Versailles useful to the whole mass of the people – the only thing that could be reached at the time. The appropriation of the Bank of France alone would have been enough to dissolve all the pretensions of the Versailles people in terror, etc., etc.... The doctrinaire and necessarily fantastic anticipations of the programme of action for a revolution of the future only divert us from the struggle of the present....

Marx's explanation of the Commune has had grave consequences. Above all, taken together with the ferocious suppression of the rising, it inspired whole generations of workers during the period of the Second International; but it did nothing to assist political clarity. Since it was described as 'the first proletarian revolution' it is understandable that Lenin, with sure political instinct, took over its tradition for the October Revolution in Russia. He took Marx's mythology of the Commune and made it the basis of the Bolshevik theory of the State. He had always been inspired by that circular letter which Marx had written in March 1850, and in which he had explained 'the permanent revolution'. Indeed Marx looked upon it as a tactical order which he countermanded a few months later, having seen that it was based on a complete misconception of the situation. This did not stop Lenin. He knew the long circular by heart and always took special pleasure in quoting it. *Permanent Revolution*, which for Marx was a tactical error, became for Lenin an essential element in Marxist theory.

12

THE UNFINISHED LIFE-WORK

The importance of the International lay in the fact that it gave the workers in different countries a greater feeling that their destinies were linked together, and produced concrete battle-cries for the political and economic struggle. These helped to educate the conscience of the socialist parties of the seventies and eighties, and they also became the battle-cries of the Second International which was founded in 1889. As far as Marx himself was concerned, the Hague Congress and the duel with Bakunin put an end to the final chapter of his political activity. He no longer took an active part, though he still felt the towering waves of political conflict to be his proper element. In his book on the Commune during the rising he thought he had discovered 'a new starting-point of the greatest importance for world history' in 'the struggle between the working class and the capitalist class and capitalist state'. For this reason it gave him very great satisfaction whenever he was attacked for supporting the Commune: 'The Address is creating a devilish amount of fuss, and "at this moment" I have the honour of being "the best calumniated and the most menaced man of London"', he wrote to his friend Kugelmann on 18 June 1871. An active participation in politics stimulated and increased his powers. So it was that during the early years of his voluminous labours for the International he also at last found the strength to complete the first part of his scientific life-work, *Capital, A Critique of Political Economy*, on which he had already been engaged for twenty years. Nothing shows more clearly the stimulating and rejuvenating effect of his political activity. But just as during the two periods of his political activity (in line with the Promethean ambitions of his youth) he set himself tasks that were beyond the strength of one man, so too in this scientific life-work of his. It too remained no more than a torso; but

The Paris Commune, spring 1871: barricades

it is a torso such that its limbs are of gigantic size and have occupied whole generations of specialist scholars.

The preliminary studies began during 1843–4, with the analyses of wages, profits and rent in the Paris *Economic and Philosophic Manuscripts*. If Marx had not considered these important as his starting-point, they would certainly never have been preserved. As early as January 1845 Engels urged him: 'See that you get your book on economics finished'; and during the next few years other friends also tried to persuade him. Parts of these early studies were used in the *German Ideology*, in the book against Proudhon, and in the *Communist Manifesto*. But his obligation to finish the book – particularly so that it could form the basis of the theory that social revolution was a necessary result of antagonism between the classes in bourgeois society – became more urgent after the end of the revolutionary period and during the squabbles with the refugees in London. In 1851 Marx thought that he would have the book ready within five weeks. The crisis of 1857 again made it desirable to finish, in order to have a basis of theory during the expected revolution. In 1859 several chapters appeared under the title *Towards a Critique of*

The remains of the victory column in the Vendôme, destroyed by the Communards as a symbol of the First Empire

Political Economy, without arousing much applause. Then Lassalle's agitation spurred him on to complete the book. But in the meantime the research material had become so voluminous that there were great difficulties about bringing the thing to an end. Although at first Marx had only been thinking in terms of a history of economic theories, the plan was continually widening. It was not possible to deduce theories from theories; he had got to study bourgeois society itself and 'its anatomy as represented by economics':

> The huge amount of material piled up in the British Museum, the favourable vantage-point that London offered for studying bourgeois society, and finally the new stage of development that seemed to have been reached with the discovery of gold in California and Australia, all obliged me to start again from the beginning and work critically through the new material. These studies seemed to lead me into quite separate branches of science, in which I was obliged to linger for varying lengths of time.

The material which Marx collected in the British Museum is to be found in several dozen notebooks, whose total volume may well be greater than the manuscript of the work itself. These notebooks provided the basis for all his sociological, historical and economic investigations.

Besides the theoretical studies there was the observation and analysis of concrete social conditions to be found in many journalistic articles.

The completion of Marx's work was delayed by many causes, by his having to earn his living, by illness, and by all the wretched conditions that beset the family. But fearful as the effect of these was (and Marx frequently inveighed against 'the damned book' that weighed on him like a mountain), these were not the principal difficulties. Nor was it even the many details of science and practical economics, on which he often had to seek Engels's advice: 'I find it the same with mechanics as with languages. I understand the mathematical laws all right, but the simplest technical reality that requires an opinion is more difficult for me than for the biggest blockheads.'

The chief difficulty lay far more in the conflict between his scientific conscience and his direct involvement as a politician. In 1851 it was possible for Marx to believe that he would be finished in five weeks, because even before 1848 he had reached a firm standpoint from which he could criticize the bourgeois economy; this was because he thought he had acquired a broad insight into the operational laws of bourgeois production. It was therefore only a question of finding some material to support his theory of the class war and social revolution. For this purpose he took up the study of economics, and there could not have been much difficulty in gathering some material quickly. The notebooks show that the search for material took a long time. But the longer Marx buried himself in questions of detail, the more complicated he saw the material to be, and as a scholar he considered it irresponsible to speak about things he did not understand completely. Then the plan of the whole work was altered a number of times. In addition there was the scholarly ethos, the interest in *truth* itself, which he defined very well in a comparison of the characters of Ricardo and Malthus. 'So far as it could be done without sinning against his scientific attitude', Ricardo always remained a philanthropist, as in fact he always was in his life; Malthus on the other hand always took great care not to offend the interests of the reactionary elements among the ruling classes, and this was mean: 'I call a man "mean" if he seeks to adjust the truth, not to something in itself (however erroneous it may be), but to certain external, alien and superficial interests.' Marx was convinced that the ruling classes showed a lack of awareness in their ideologies and that only the proletariat could have a true awareness. For that very reason this view of scientific truth always made him aware of the threatened conflict between interests (even

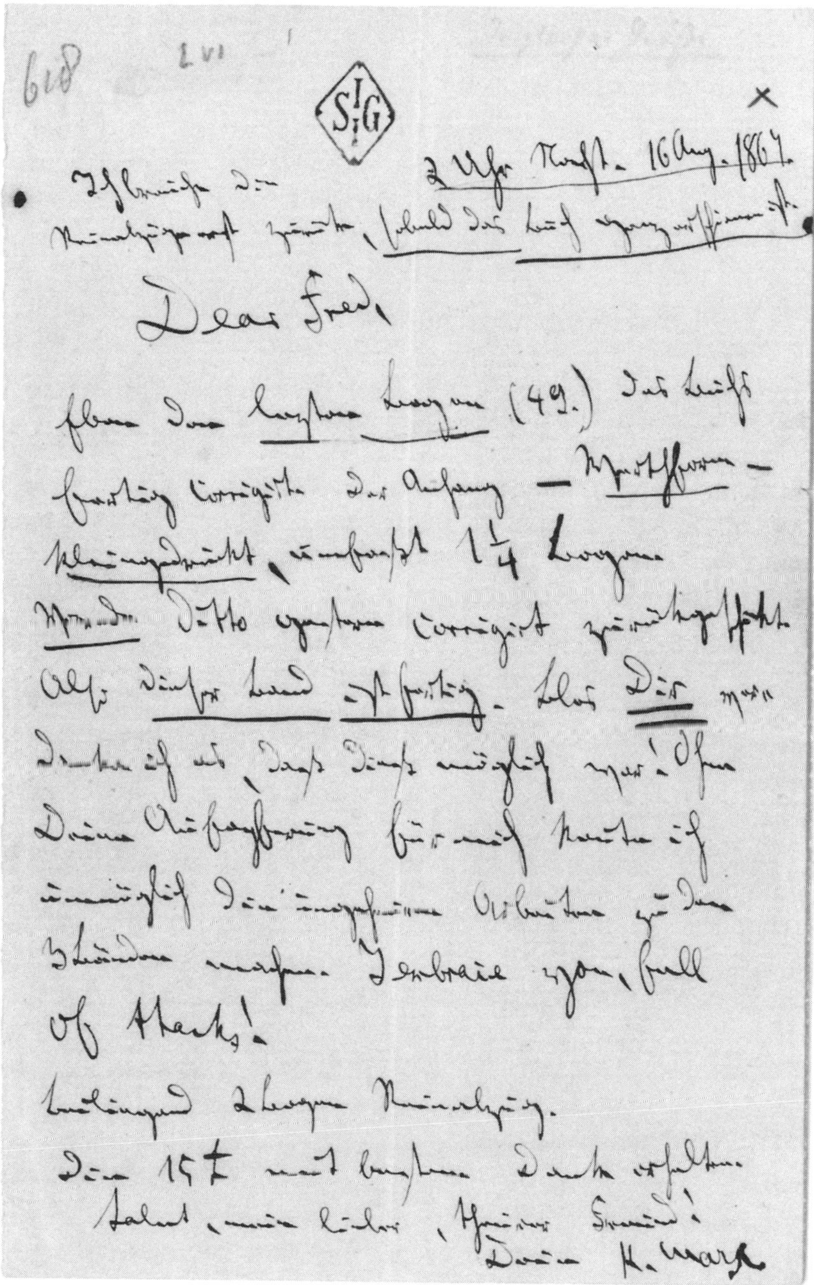

Ich brauche die Reinabzüge zurück, sobald das Buch ausgeschienen ist.

2 Uhr Nachts. 16 Aug. 1867.

Dear Fred,

Eben den letzten Bogen (49.) des Buchs fertig corrigirt. Der Anhang – Werthform – kleingedruckt, umfasst 1 1/4 Bogen.

Vorrede ditto gestern corrigirt zurückgeschickt. Also dieser Band ist fertig. Blos Dir verdanke ich es, dass diess möglich war! Ohne Deine Aufopferung für mich konnte ich unmöglich die ungeheuren Arbeiten zu den 3 Bänden machen. I embrace you, full of thanks!

Beiliegend 2 Bogen Reinabzug.

Die 15 £ mit bestem Dank erhalten.

Salut, mein lieber, theurer Freund!

Dein K. Marx

Marx's letter thanking Engels for correcting the proofs of *Capital* proletarian interests) and the search for truth. Many discordancies and contradictions, which seem to exist in his work, may well stem from this.

Even the great work which Marx was able to publish in 1867 is only a fraction of his life-work on economics. The greater part he left behind him in a series of fragments, out of which Engels 'was supposed to make something'. Engels was horrified at the condition of the manuscript, which after Marx's repeated assurances he had always thought was completed. Engels devoted most of the rest of his life to editing the papers, and was able to publish the second volume in 1885 and the third in 1894. From 1905 to 1910 Karl Kautsky published four volumes entitled *Theories on Surplus Value*, though again even this was only a part of the available manuscript on the subject. On several occasions fragments were published, the most important (preliminary studies from the years 1857–8) being issued in Moscow in 1939 under the title *Outlines of the Critique of Political Economy* (the *Grundrisse*). There is a varied literature dealing with the contradictions between the first and the later volumes, and about the alteration in the plan of the whole work. These are all theoretical statements about the existing texts, intended to refute or offer some excuse for Marx's views. Hitherto no real investigation has been undertaken to examine the sources critically; only by this means could it be discovered how far Engels really worked over the later volumes and whether it was actually only quite a small proportion of the Marx manuscripts that he decided to ignore.

It was only after Marx's death that his economic theories began to exert a historical influence in the disputes within the working-class movement and the specialist branches of science. Then the effect of the labour theory of value and the theory of surplus value, the theories of concentration and accumulation, of exploitation and pauperization, the theories of crisis and collapse, of class war and revolution began to be felt. A number of the theories were already being violently disputed amongst the workers at the turn of the century, while others were held to be stages of development rather than absolutely valid theories. Today many individual items in these theories play a part in the most recent economic ideas. It is therefore necessary that *Capital* should be assigned its proper place in Marx's life-work and in his total conception.

For a few generations of the workers it was enough for them to be certain that socialism would be achieved 'with the inevitability of a natural process' and that the hour would come when the expropriators would be expropriated. Their understanding of Marx was based on the

Das Kapital.

Kritik der politischen Oekonomie.

Von

Karl Marx.

Erster Band.

Buch I: Der Produktionsprocess des Kapitals.

Das Recht der Uebersetzung wird vorbehalten.

Hamburg
Verlag von Otto Meissner.
1867.

New-York: L. W. Schmidt. 24 Barclay-Street.

Title-page of the first volume of *Capital*

Communist Manifesto and on the first volume of *Capital*, which Engels christened 'the Workers' Bible'. They knew the book from countless popularizations in many different languages, which adapted Marx's difficult thought processes to the understanding of the simplest man. But generally they were content with the certainty that Marx had proved the inevitability of the end of bourgeois society and the victory of socialism. This inevitability was also economically determined according to the official theory. Hence Marx's *Capital* was considered to be his real work, and his earlier writings were looked upon as immature early stages in his life-work that were soon superseded. This view was opposed by a different one, borne out by the Early Writings, to the effect that Marx's entire conception had already been visible from the forties onwards. So, when he began his economic studies, he was interested in getting a clear idea of the position occupied by the proletariat in bourgeois society. Henceforth he was guided by the notion, revealed by his criticism of Hegel, that man had degenerated and become alienated from his true being; moreover that this alienation had reached its peak in the industry based on competition and the division of labour, and that man would only be able to recover his true being through a universal emancipation to be achieved through social revolution. There was ample evidence in *Capital* for all the individual elements in the conception; but its importance can only be adequately judged within the framework of this conception.

Marx's attitude became more 'realistic', and it was more concerned with 'events' than with man himself, who had always held the centre of the stage in the early work. An attempt had been made to explain this by his strong preoccupation with economics, that sober and unemotional science. Moreover there was the fact that he stressed the inevitable slow process of development, achieved without the co-operation of man. This seems to be in contrast with Marx's frequent expectations of revolution, which support the assumption that he considered the social conflicts adequate for successful revolution. Furthermore the 'objectivity' of his views might be ascribed to political disappointments, above all the disappointment of his revolutionary hopes, and of course to the conditions in which he lived. Marx's language also became harsher and more sober. But it is not really probable that he was ashamed of the anthropology of his youth; for one can detect unmistakably that it was always very real to him. And if his theories were interpreted either in a vulgarly materialist sense or with an exaggerated economic determinism and automatism, he could always say humorously: 'As for me, I am no Marxist.'

When integrating *Capital* into that early conception one must be careful to avoid making the same kind of mistake that used to be made in viewing Marx as a 'pure economist' – namely the mistake of thinking that the young philosopher was the true Marx, while the old Marx had become decadent and paralysed. Anyone who takes the trouble to study Marx's development will see clearly that there can be no question of any such split. In the first place there is the abstract consideration that all the elements in Marx's thought were always united in his consciousness and that no intellectual impulse was ever lost. But it is also obvious that when the critique of his philosophical past led Marx on to the anthropological sociology of real humanism, he absorbed socio-economic events into his thinking, where they were blended with earlier elements. They became the fertile soil on which his sociology thrived. All categories in his thought are simultaneously philosophic *and* economic categories. Politics constituted an additional element; and he fell under the sway of politics from the moment when he realized that it was not simply a question of interpreting the world, but of *changing* it. If we survey Marx's life, we cannot doubt that it was this impulse which in the last resort dominated this honest and passionate thinker. We have no need of Engels's testimony that Marx was 'more than half' a politician; nor that of the Russian sociologist Maxim Kovalevsky, speaking of the 'old' Marx, though his testimony is typical of many:

> The most astonishing thing about Marx was his passionate partisanship in all political questions. It was scarcely in keeping with the calm objective method which he recommended to his followers and which was supposed to investigate all phenomena according to the assumptions of economics.

Marx, on the other hand, insisted on amalgamating politics, philosophy and economics. And it is this very fusion that produces the problem of the relationship between idea and reality, between theory and practice. It runs right through Marx's life as well as through the history of Marxist thought and socialist politics, and it occupies a central position in the discussion between Marxist critics.

13

THE FINALE AND POSTHUMOUS FAME

The view that after 1872 Marx was really 'a dead man' is certainly false. He was in the evening of his life; he had reached the age of fifty-five. More and more now he lived the life of a tranquil scholar. Maxim Kovalevsky portrays him at this time:

> People still think of Marx as a gloomy and arrogant rebel against bourgeois science and bourgeois culture. But in reality Marx was a highly cultivated gentleman of the Anglo-German pattern. Intimate relations with Heine had endowed him with a cheerful disposition and a capacity for witty satire. Thanks to the fact that the conditions of his personal life were now as favourable as possible, he was a happy man.

After Engels moved to London in 1870, personal relations between them were very animated. Poverty was no longer a factor in Marx's life, since Engels had amply provided for him; and this torment, which had produced many others, was now at an end. Of course Marx and his wife often suffered from illness, as we know; but now at least convalescence was easier for them. The daughters Jenny and Laura married the French socialists Charles Longuet and Paul Lafargue respectively, and they and the parents were on good terms. Grandchildren were growing up; and Helene Demuth still continued to keep house.

For several decades Marx had complained about the 'conspiracy of silence' against his books, but now his name had become known in scientific circles. A second German edition of *Capital* was published, as well as a French and a Russian translation. Moreover his name appeared more frequently in the socialist newspapers; it became more familiar to the workers, although it was not until the eighties that his ideas really began to make triumphant progress. Marx worked as indefatigably as ever; but his work consisted chiefly of amassing a huge number of excerpts, without however making any use of them. He completed a

Jenny and her husband Charles Longuet

detailed chronology of world history, based on the work of Schlosser, chiefly in order to refresh his memory. He made excerpts freely from books on agrarian questions, chemistry, geology, primeval history, banking and monetary questions, and he studied mathematics, mostly with a view to showing the relationship between surplus value and profits. He was particularly interested in all Russian affairs, and he learnt Russian in order to find out about Russian statistics, about the work of the tax commission and about agrarian questions. As regards original work, in addition to the *Critique of the Gotha Programme* he wrote a contribution to Engels's *Anti-Dühring*. From a political point of view Marx must have received considerable satisfaction. He communicated with political friends in many different countries and gave them his advice. He saw the power of Anarchism dwindle slowly. He was pleased at the electoral successes of the German Social Democrats, and he drafted an electoral programme for the French socialists which contained up-to-date demands for the

Laura's husband,
Paul Lafargue

workers. During this period there are a number of milder statements about future developments, such as the one addressed to the Russian sociologist Mikhailovsky and contained in the letter to Vera Zasulich, to the effect that there is more than one path leading to socialism. He quoted from *Capital* a passage saying that all Western European countries must inevitably follow the sort of capitalist line of development taken by England, and remarked that he had 'deliberately restricted the historical inevitability of this line of development to the countries of Western Europe'. As early as 1872, in a speech in Amsterdam on the subject of revolution, he said that revolution was not inevitable in England, and perhaps not in Holland and certain other countries.

Marx and his daughter Jenny

The death of his wife Jenny on 2 December 1881 dealt Marx a blow from which he never really recovered. His health deteriorated:

> I have emerged from my last illness crippled in a twofold manner: morally through the death of my wife, and physically because I am left with a thickening of the pleura and an increased sensitivity of the trachea. I shall have to completely sacrifice a certain amount of time in various manoeuvres to restore my health.

During 1882 he stayed in France, Algiers and Switzerland; and he was not at home for more than a few weeks. A rapid decay in his physical and mental powers set in. His letters give minute descriptions of his condition. The letters of this time show a change in him quite as great as that revealed in the last picture from Algiers. The letters show us the fatigued state of this great mind. On 31 March he wrote to Engels:

> *Mon cher*, like other family members you'll be struck by the mistakes in my spelling and bad grammar. It strikes me too – even though I'm so muddled – but only *post festum*. Shows you there's something in *sana mens in sano corpore*...

On 20 May he complained: 'How pointless and empty life is, but how desirable!' On 11 January 1883 his daughter Jenny Longuet died suddenly, and on 14 March Marx himself died.

Engels had been in no doubt about his condition:

> Perhaps medical skill might have been able to procure him a few more years of vegetative existence, the life of a helpless creature. It might have been a triumph for the doctors that he did not die suddenly, but instead he would have died by inches. And our poor Marx could never have borne that. To go on living with so many uncompleted tasks ahead of him, with a tantalizing desire to finish them and yet without the ability to do it – that would have been a thousand times more bitter for him than the peaceful death that overtook him. He was accustomed to say with Epicurus that Death is no misfortune for the one who dies, but only for the one who survives. And to have to watch this powerful man of genius linger on as a ruin, for the greater glory of medicine and as an object of scorn to the Philistines, whom he had so often defeated in his strength – no, it is a thousand times better as it is....

Marx was destined never to know that in all the countries of Europe democratic mass parties were coming to acknowledge him. When the Zürich Congress of the Second International in 1893 gave a wild ovation to Friedrich Engels (who had been invited to the closing session by Bebel), Engels was deeply moved: 'If only Marx had been able to stand beside me and see this!'

Marx's wife in the last years of her life

For several generations of workers Marx was the symbol of their hopes for a life worthy of humanity – a life free from want or anxiety. Wherever the battle-cry of the *Communist Manifesto* rang out, the workers followed it. Marx's theories strengthened their class consciousness, inspired them in their struggles for political and economic rights, and directed their thoughts towards the supreme aims of humanity. For the working classes of the whole civilized world the movement founded on his doctrines embodied the very greatest cultural value; within this movement they fought to win their place in society. Without this movement the history of the past century and indeed our whole civilization is unthinkable.

For the most part little was known of Marx's theories. But that little was enough to exert a magical power on the workers, leading them to withstand the enemy. To find comparisons for the effect of these doctrines one has to look to the history of religion. For his followers these doctrines were a source of faith: Marx gave them a sense of certainty which absolutely excluded any doubts in his view of the course of history. He gave an assurance of ultimate victory.

But since Marx's doctrines became the theory of a movement, they were bound to change into dogmas and an ideology. And since Marx's theories also depended on the validity of his concept of history, contradictions were bound to appear between these and the progressive development that corrected them. The theories had to be explained and indeed, since canonical writings cannot be interpolated, reality had to be touched up in order to preserve agreement. Of course the supporters of the 'true doctrine' called themselves orthodox. But wherever there is an orthodoxy, there are also those who doubt. They were decried, and later they were 'traitors to the working class'. What an absurd contradiction this was to Marx's slogan of *De omnibus dubitandum*, which made the heresy of doubt positively obligatory! And no theory can remain vital amid dynamic reality, if it does not acquire fresh certainty from doubt.

If we ask what the situation is with Marx's ideas today, we shall often be told that their effectiveness is really over. And there is substantial evidence to back this. Even if one recognizes that Marxist theory forecast quite accurately a number of developments in industrial society, it must be admitted that this theory drew some completely incorrect conclusions from the analysis of society. In spite of the social conflicts which Marx pointed out, no general collapse ensued, although society was repeatedly shattered by the most severe wars and crises. Again, in Marx's view Russia was the one country in which it would not be possible for social revolution to be achieved. It is certain that a doubt of the correctness of Marx's view – we are not talking about certain of his individual predictions (they do not count, for he was no prophet) – is causing great masses of people to give the same answer. That answer becomes easier for those who feel that Marx's ideas are inappropriate and untimely amidst the prosperous conditions that surround them. Another group sought for God in the religion of the State, which is also associated with Marx's name, and this group was disappointed when their search proved fruitless. Here is another answer: even if one defines freedom as 'a recognition of necessity', it is nevertheless completely absurd to describe freedom as a recognition of the necessity of absence-of-freedom, of State absolutism and dictatorship. There are a whole number of motives for giving a negative answer to the question of whether Marx's ideas are still valid.

On the other hand it is only now that the proper time has come for Western scholarship to carry out a detailed and full-scale examination of

The last photograph of Marx, Algiers, April 1882

Marx and his ideas. Nowadays Marx and his theories are an outstanding subject of research for philosophers and sociologists, historians and economists. It is astonishing what a thorough examination is made of even the most insignificant aspects of Marxism. And it is not only the attention paid towards the East that stimulates research. The philosophy of the present day, in so far as it looks towards the future, is founded on a real humanism or at least by no means ignores it. It finds points of contact in the attitude of the young Marx, since it deals with human existence as a whole.

The history of the development of Marx's theories, the history of 'Marxism', ceases to be a matter of the biography of Marx. His ideas, as they worked themselves out historically, became separated from their creator and came to lead a life of their own, exuberant and distorted. Marxism is not his creation; the person chiefly responsible for this was Karl Kautsky. Marxism split up into many different schools and

The grave at Highgate Cemetery

tendencies; and nothing proves so conclusively the many-sided quality of Marx's life-work as the fact that all the different tendencies base themselves on Marx and that they are all entitled to do so. This is true of the orthodox followers and the revisionists of all shades, just as it is true of the Bolsheviks. And it even applies to those heretics who (on the lines of Marx's own view of history) felt that the dilemma of socialist theory and of the socialist movement lay in the danger that ideas might become rigidified into an ideology, and who saw the discrepancy between theory and practice as an ever-recurring problem. And it is precisely by stating this problem as clearly as possible that they can be sure of earning the fullest possible agreement from Marx himself. In the preparatory studies for his doctoral dissertation Marx himself said that it was necessary that Hegel's ideology should be analysed. He did not consider it in any way a desecration that the philosophy of his great teacher, the creator of the 'world-philosophy', should be subjected to detailed criticism.

Marx's attitude towards politics repeatedly presents the observer with this problem, one that becomes all the more urgent in view of the fact that he was such a passionately involved politician. What was his relationship to reality? How were his broad views linked with it in political action? Did he really demonstrate the unity between the philosopher and the politician? These problems cannot be solved in an abstract and dialectical fashion; the solutions can only be given concretely in detailed analyses. Moreover in the process, since the thinker and politician is ultimately a living man, his supreme subjectivity should on no account be overlooked.

CHRONOLOGY

1818	5 May: Karl Marx born in Trier.
1835	Matriculation examination at the Friedrich-Wilhelm Gymnasium in Trier. Law student at Bonn.
1836	Betrothal to Jenny von Westphalen. Studies in Berlin. Literary efforts.
1837	Frequents the 'Post-Graduate Club', with the Bauer brothers, Buhl, Köppen, Mayer, Ruttenberg, and others.
1838	On 10 May his father Heinrich Marx dies. He quarrels with his family.
1841	15 April: takes his degree *in absentia* at Jena.
1842	Contributes to the *Rheinische Zeitung*, and after 15 October becomes editor. Becomes friendly with Ruge.
1843	18 March: ceases to be editor. 12 June: he is married in Kreuznach. At the end of October he arrives in Paris.
1844	*Deutsch-französische Jahrbücher*. Quarrels with Ruge. *Economic and Philosophical Manuscripts*. Association with Heine and Proudhon. 1 May: his first daughter, Jenny, is born. At the end of August Friedrich Engels comes to visit Marx for ten days, and from then onwards they collaborate closely.
1845	*The Holy Family*. 3 February: arrives in Brussels after being expelled from France. July–August: travels to England with Engels for research. At the end of the year he begins work on *The German Ideology*.
1846	The Communist Correspondence Committee. 30 March: dispute with Weitling. Association with Harney, Weerth, Weydemeyer and Wolff. Birth of his daughter Laura.
1847	*Poverty of Philosophy*. Member of the Communist League. At

the beginning of December takes part in the Second Congress of the League in London. *Deutsche Brüsseler Zeitung*. Birth of his son Edgar.

1848 February: *Communist Manifesto*. Beginning of March: expelled from Belgium. 10 April: arrives in Cologne. 31 May: first number of the *Neue Rheinische Zeitung*; Marx is chief editor. Dissolution of the Communist League.

1849 Acquitted in a trial for 'incitement to rebellion'. 16 May: expelled as a stateless subject. 18 May: final number of the newspaper. 3 June: in Paris. 24 August: begins his exile in London. End of October: birth of his son Guido (died 19 November 1851).

1850 Refounding of the Communist League. *Neue Rheinische Zeitung. Politisch-ökonomische Revue*. The League is split up.

1851 Economic studies. Begins his association with *The New York Tribune*.

1852 *The Eighteenth Brumaire of Louis Bonaparte*, *The Great Men of Exile*. Association with Bangya. Trial of Communists in Cologne. The League is finally dissolved.

1853 *Revelations on the Communist Trial in Cologne*.

1855 Contributes to the *Neue Oder-Zeitung*. 16 January: birth of his daughter Eleanor. 6 April: death of his son Edgar.

1859 *A Contribution to the Critique of Political Economy*. Contributes to the London *People*.

1860 *Herr Vogt*.

1861 March–April: visits Lassalle in Berlin. Contributes to the Vienna *Presse*.

1863 Lassalle's agitation. 30 November: death of his mother Henriette Marx.

1864 9 May: death of Wilhelm Wolff. 31 August: death of Ferdinand Lassalle. 28 September: Meeting at which the Working Men's International Association is founded. 24 November: Address and Provisional Rules of the International.

1865 Breach with the Union of German Workers. *Value, Price and Profit*. Conference of the International in London.

1866 First Congress of the International in Geneva.

1867 First volume of *Capital*. Second Congress in Lausanne.

1868 Third Congress of the International in Brussels. Bakunin's

	International Alliance.
1869	Fourth Congress of the International in Basle. Congress held at Eisenach of the Party of Social Democratic Workers. 'Confidential communication' regarding Bakunin.
1870	Addresses the General Council of the International on the Franco-Prussian War. Engels moves to London.
1871	The Paris Commune. *The Civil War in France*. Contributes to the Leipzig *Volksstaat*. Conference of the International in London.
1872	Last Congress of the International at The Hague. Exclusion of Bakunin. Transfer of the General Council to New York.
1875	German workers' parties united at Gotha: Socialist Workers' Party. *Critique of the Gotha Programme*.
1876	Death of Mikhail Bakunin.
1877	Collaborates with Engels on *Anti-Dühring*.
1878	Anti-Socialist Law passed in Germany.
1881	2 December: death of his wife Jenny Marx.
1882	Travels to Algiers, Switzerland and France.
1883	11 January: death of his daughter Jenny Longuet. 14 March: death of Karl Marx.
1885	Second volume of *Capital*.
1890	Death of Helene Demuth.
1894	Third volume of *Capital*.
1895	Death of Friedrich Engels.
1905–10	*Theories on Surplus Value*.
1913	*The Correspondence between Friedrich Engels and Karl Marx* published.
1927	*The Marx–Engels Collected Edition* begins to appear.
1932	*Historical Materialism*, and the Early Writings published.
1939	*Grundrisse der Kritik der Politischen Ökonomie* published.

OPINIONS

Max Weber

We have deliberately avoided proving what seems to us far and away the most important instance of the construction of ideal-types: namely, Marx. We shall ... only note here that naturally all specifically Marxist 'laws' and developmental structures – in so far as they are theoretically correct – have the character of an ideal type. The pre-eminent, indeed the unique heuristic importance of these ideal types, if one uses them to make a comparison with reality, and equally the great danger of them as soon as they are represented as being empirically valid or even real (i.e. actually metaphysical) 'operative forces', 'tendencies', etc., is known to anyone who has ever worked with Marxist concepts.

'Objectivity' in Social and Political Knowledge, 1904

George Bernard Shaw

Moreover, twenty-five years ago it was fashionable in English socialist circles to say that one had read Karl Marx and Friedrich Engels (a fashion still, as they say, all the rage in Germany among older Social Democrats), and I read the famous first volume of *Das Kapital* too, only to discover that nobody else had, and that it contained not a word about what socialism was. But I consider that Marx was not really an author – either German or any other nationality. He was an anti-bourgeois and his battle cry was, 'Anti-bourgeois of all countries, unite to fight', which they still do every three years. The world is greatly indebted to Marx for his description of the selfishness and stupidity of that respected middle class so worshipped in Germany and England, and *Das Kapital* is one of those books that changes people if they can be persuaded to read it. However, it is the work of a man who was not a member of normal German or English society and who wrote about capitalists and workers like a class-war correspondent.

What I Owe German Culture, 1911

Joseph Schumpeter

He did not only possess originality but also scientific ability of the highest order. An idea like the one that modern income from interest is in essence similar to the rent of the feudal landlord – whether right or wrong – marks its author as a man of scientific talent even if he never had another idea. Theoretical analysis was second nature to him and he never tired of working out its details. This fact also contributes to his success in Germany. At the time when his first volume appeared there was nobody in Germany who could have measured himself against him either in vigour of thought or in theoretical knowledge.

Economic Doctrine and Method, 1924

Revolution or evolution? If I have caught Marx's meaning, the answer is not hard to give. Evolution was for him the parent of socialism. He was much too strongly imbued with a sense of the inherent logic of things social to believe that revolution can replace any part of the work of evolution. The revolution comes in nevertheless. But it only comes in order to write the conclusion under a complete set of premises. The Marxian revolution therefore differs entirely, in nature and in function, from the revolutions both of the bourgeois radical and of the socialist conspirator. It is essentially revolution in the fullness of time. It is true that disciples who dislike this conclusion, and especially its application to the Russian case, can point to many passages in the sacred books that seem to contradict it. But in those passages Marx himself contradicts his deepest and most mature thought which speaks out unmistakably from the analytic structure of *Das Kapital* and – as any thought must that is inspired by a sense of the inherent logic of things – carries, beneath the fantastic glitter of dubious gems, a distinctly conservative implication. And, after all, why not? No serious argument ever supports any 'ism' unconditionally. To say that Marx, stripped of phrases, admits of interpretation in a conservative sense is only saying that he can be taken seriously.

Capitalism, Socialism, and Democracy, 1943

Werner Sombart

However harshly I reject the *Weltanschauung* of this man, and with it everything that is comprehensively and proudly described today as 'Marxism', I do admire him heartily as the theoretician and historian of capitalism. And everything that is of any value in my work is due to the spirit of Marx. Marx's greatest genius was his masterly understanding of how to frame questions. Even today we are still living on these questions of his. By posing these questions of genius he has mapped out for economic science a whole century of fruitful research. Any social economist, who did not know how to absorb these questions, was condemned to barrenness; and this is something we can say with certainty today.

Modern Capitalism, 1928

Eugen Schmalenbach

What are the real reasons that oblige us to leave the old free economy in spite of its extraordinary efficiency, and move on to a new economy with a fixed form, when we still know very little about its productive efficiency? The first thing that should be said is that this is not a matter of a deliberate decision. Those who direct the economy have not set themselves the aim of abandoning the old economic system and trying a new one. None of our economic leaders is entering on this new economic system of his own free will. It is not free men, but strong economic forces that are driving us on into the new economic epoch. It can even be said that almost all our economic leaders are, at least theoretically, outspoken opponents of the economic ideas that provide the foundation for the new economic system. What is it basically that we are now experiencing, if it is not the fulfilment of the prophecies of the great socialist Marx? It is his ideas about the future of the economy that we are now seeing being fulfilled. If we were to tell the economic leaders of today that, willingly or unwillingly, they are so to speak the executors of Marx's last will and testament, they would, I assume, deny it emphatically. No, one really cannot say that our economic leaders are deliberately forcing us into the new fixed economy. They are tools, nothing but tools. And if we inquire about the real causes for the change of system, then we must seek these causes not in men, but in things.

1928

Othmar Spann

Today's so-called bourgeois economic and sociological theory, indeed even the theory of history too, are so completely dominated by the basic ideas of Marx that they only differ from the Marxist theories by a matter of degree.

1930

Stefan Zweig

It was at the University that I first got to know the work of Karl Marx; and I found it a blessing, after all the abstract interpretations of the world, such as those of Hegel and Schelling, to find at last an intellectual work which looked straight at life, and took its material not from History but from the Future. The wonderful compelling logic, the merciless diagnosis, and above all the prophetic way of posing a problem, all made a most profound impression on me, and I felt deeply the dynamic power concentrated in these few hundred pages.

Answer to a questionnaire in *International Literature*, 1933

Sigmund Freud

There are assertions contained in Marx's theory which have struck me as strange: such as that the development of forms of society is a process of natural history, or that the changes in social stratification arise from one another in the manner of a dialectical process. I am far from sure that I understand these assertions aright; nor do they sound to me 'materialistic' but, rather, like a precipitate of obscure Hegelian philosophy in whose school Marx graduated. I do not know how I can shake off my lay opinion that the class structure of society goes back to the struggles which, from the beginning of history, took place between human hordes only slightly differing from each other. Social distinctions, so I thought, were originally distinctions between clans or races....

The strength of Marxism clearly lies, not in its view of history or the prophecies of the future that are based on it, but in its sagacious indication of the decisive influence which the economic circumstances of men have upon their intellectual, ethical and artistic attitudes. A number of connections and implications were thus uncovered which had previously been almost totally overlooked. But it cannot be assumed that economic motives are the only ones that determine the behaviour of human beings in society. The undoubted fact that different individuals, races and nations behave differently under the same economic conditions is alone enough to show that economic motives are not the sole dominating factors. It is altogether incomprehensible how psychological factors can be overlooked where what is in question are the reactions of living human beings.

New Introductory Lectures on Psycho-Analysis, 1933

Georg Lukács

Over thirty years have passed since, as a boy, I first read the *Communist Manifesto*. A progressive – but not continuous (however contradictory this may sound) – absorption in the works of Marx has in fact made up the history of my intellectual development; more than that, it has even been the history of my whole life, in so far as this has been of any importance for society. It seems to me that in the epoch that followed the appearance of Marx, the task of coming to terms with him was bound to form the central problem for any thinker who took himself at all seriously. I feel that the manner and extent to which Marx's methods and results have been appropriated really determine his place in human development.

My Road to Marx, 1933

BIBLIOGRAPHY

Collected Editions

Marx, K., and Engels, F., *Historisch-kritische Gesamtausgabe. Werke, Schriften, Briefe*, 12 vols, edited at the Marx–Engels Institute, Moscow, by David Riazanov, 1927–35. Generally cited as MEGA (*Marx/Engels Gesamtausgabe*).

Marx, K. and Engels, F., *Werke*, 41 vols, edited by the Institute for Marxism–Leninism, Berlin (East), 1956–68.

Selections

Selected Works, 1 vol., London, 1968.

On Religion, London, 1955.

On Colonialism, London, 1959.

On Britain, London, 1962.

On Colonialism and Modernization, edited by Shlomo Avineri, New York, 1968.

The Essential Marx, edited by Ernst Fischer and Franz Marek, New York and London, 1971.

Selected Writings in Sociology and Social Philosophy, edited by T.B. Bottomore and Maximilien Rubel, London, 1956; New York, 1964.

Early Writings, edited by T.B. Bottomore, London, 1963; New York, 1964.

Writings of the Young Marx on Philosophy and Society, edited by Loyd D. Easton and Kurt H. Guddat, New York, 1967.

Early Texts, edited by David McLellan, Oxford, 1971.

Separate Works

(*listed in the order in which they were written*)

The Difference between the Democritean and Epicurean Philosophy of Nature (Marx's doctoral dissertation), in Norman D. Livergood, *Activity in Marx's Philosophy*, The Hague, 1967.

Critique of Hegel's 'Philosophy of Right', edited by Joseph O' Malley, Cambridge, 1970.

The Holy Family, London, 1956.
The Poverty of Philosophy, New York, 1963.
The German Ideology, London and New York, 1965.
The German Ideology, part 1 with selections from parts 2 and 3, edited by C.J. Arthur, London, 1971.
Manifesto of the Communist Party, Moscow and London, no date.
Wage-Labour and Capital, Moscow and London, 1970.
The Class Struggles in France, 1848 to 1850, Moscow and London, 1965.
The Eighteenth Brumaire of Louis Bonaparte, Moscow and London, 1967.
The Secret Diplomatic History of the Eighteenth Century, edited by Lester Hutchinson, London, 1969.
The Cologne Trials, introduction by Rodney Livingstone, London, 1971.
A Contribution to the Critique of Political Economy, introduction by Maurice Dobb, London, 1971.
Value, Price and Profit: addressed to working men, edited by Eleanor Marx Aveling, London, 1951.
Pre-Capitalist Economic Formations (a section from the *Grundrisse*), edited by Eric Hobsbawm, London, 1964.
Marx's Grundrisse (selections), edited by David McLellan, London, 1971.
Capital, 3 vols, Moscow, 1961–62.
Capital, vol. 1, London, 1970.
Theories of Surplus Value, 2 vols, Moscow and London, 1963, 1968.
The Civil War in France, Peking, 1966.
The Critique of the Gotha Programme, Moscow and London, 1970.

Correspondence

Correspondence 1846–1895, selection, with commentary and notes, by Dona Torr, London, 1934.
Selected Correspondence, London, 1965.
Letters to Americans, New York, 1953.
Letters to Dr Kugelmann, London, 1934.

Biographical Works

Berlin, I., *Karl Marx. His Life and Environment*, revised edition, London, 1970.
Carr, E.H., *Karl Marx. A Study in Fanaticism*, London, 1934.
Collins, H. and Abramsky, C., *Karl Marx and the British Labour Movement*, London, 1965.
Cornu, A., *Karl Marx et Friedrich Engels, leur vie et leur oeuvre*, 4 vols so far covering the years 1818 to 1846, Paris, 1955–.
Gemkow, H., *Karl Marx. A Biography*, Dresden, 1968.
Kettle, A., *Karl Marx, Founder of Modern Communism*, a biography for younger readers, London, 1963.
Korsch, K., *Karl Marx*, London, 1938.
Lenin, V.I., *Karl Marx*, Peking, 1967.
Maenchen-Helfen, O. and Nicolaevsky, B., *Karl Marx: Man and Fighter*, London, 1936.

Mayer, G., *Friedrich Engels*, London, 1936.
McLellan, D., *The Young Hegelians and Karl Marx*, London, 1969.
Mehring, F., *Karl Marx, the Story of His Life*, London, 1951.
Riazanov, D., *Karl Marx, Man, Thinker and Revolutionist*, London, 1927.
Stepanova, J.A., *Karl Marx*, Moscow, 1962.
Tsuzuki, C., *The Life of Eleanor Marx, 1855–1898*, Oxford, 1967.
Reminiscences of Marx, Moscow, no date.

Theoretical Studies

Adams, H.P., *Karl Marx in His Earlier Writings*, London, 1965.
Althusser, L., *For Marx*, London, 1969.
Althusser, L., *Reading Capital*, London, 1971.
Avineri, S., *The Social and Political Thought of Karl Marx*, Cambridge, 1970.
Bober, M.M., *Karl Marx's Interpretation of History*, New York, 1965.
Boudin, L., *The Economic Doctrine of Karl Marx*, New York, 1905.
Bucharin, N., *Historical Materialism*, London, 1926.
Demetz, P., *Marx, Engels and the Poets*, London, 1967.
Dobb, M., *Studies in the Development of Capitalism*, London, 1963.
Dunayevskaya, R., *Marxism and Freedom*, New York, 1968.
Fetscher, I., *Marx and Marxism*, New York, 1971.
Fischer, E., *Marx in His Own Words*, London, 1971.
Garaudy, R., *Marxism in the Twentieth Century*, London, 1970.
Goldmann, L., *The Human Sciences and Philosophy*, London, 1969.
Hook, S., *From Hegel to Marx*, New York, 1962.
Kamenka, E., *The Ethical Foundations of Marxism*, London, 1962.
Kautsky, K., *The Dictatorship of the Proletariat*, Ann Arbor, 1964.
Kolakowski, L., *Marxism and Beyond*, London, 1968.
Korsch, K., *Marxism and Philosophy*, London, 1970.
Lange, O., *The Political Economy of Socialism*, The Hague, 1958.
Lefebvre, H., *Dialectical Materialism*, London, 1968.
Lichtheim, G., *From Marx to Hegel*, New York and London, 1971.
Löwith, K., *From Hegel to Nietzsche*, London, 1965.
Lukács, G., *History and Class Consciousness*, London, 1971.
Mandel, E., *Marxist Economic Theory*, 2 vols, London, 1967.
Mandel, E., *The Formation of the Economic Thought of Karl Marx*, London, 1971.
Mattick, P., *Marx and Keynes*, London, 1971.
Marcuse, H., *Reason and Revolution*, London, 1970.
Mayer, A.G., *Marxism: The Unity of Theory and Practice*, Cambridge, MA, 1963.
Meszárós, I., *Marx's Theory of Alienation*, London, 1971.
Plekhanov, G.V., *Fundamental Problems of Marxism*, London, 1967.
Robinson, J., *An Essay on Marxian Economics*, London, 1966.
Schmidt, A., *The Concept of Nature in Marx*, London, 1971.
Schumpeter, J.A., *Capitalism, Socialism and Democracy*, London, 1943.
Sweezy, P.M., *The Theory of Capitalist Development*, New York, 1968.

INDEX

References to illustrations are in italics after the references to the text; only illustration references are listed for Karl Marx